The Morgan Kaufmann Series in Data Management Systems
Series Editor, Jim Gray

The Object Database Standard: ODMG-93 (Release 1.2)
Edited by R. G. G. Cattell

Joe Celko's SQL for Smarties: Advanced SQL Programming
Joe Celko

Migrating Legacy Systems: Gateways, Interfaces, and the Incremental Approach
Michael Brodie and Michael Stonebraker

Database: Principles, Programming, and Performance
Patrick O'Neil

Database Modeling and Design: The Fundamental Principles, Second Edition
Toby J. Teorey

Readings in Database Systems, Second Edition
Edited by Michael Stonebraker

Atomic Transactions
Nancy Lynch, Michael Merritt, William Weihl, and Alan Fekete

Query Processing for Advanced Database Systems
Edited by Johann Christoph Freytag, David Maier, and Gottfried Vossen

Transaction Processing: Concepts and Techniques
Jim Gray and Andreas Reuter

Understanding the New SQL: A Complete Guide
Jim Melton and Alan R. Simon

Building an Object-Oriented Database System: The Story of O_2
Edited by François Bancilhon, Claude Delobel, and Paris Kanellakis

Database Transaction Models for Advanced Applications
Edited by Ahmed K. Elmagarmid

A Guide to Developing Client/Server SQL Applications
Setrag Khoshafian, Arvola Chan, Anna Wong, and Harry K. T. Wong

The Benchmark Handbook for Database and Transaction Processing Systems, Second Edition
Edited by Jim Gray

Camelot and Avalon: A Distributed Transaction Facility
Edited by Jeffrey L. Eppinger, Lily B. Mummert, and Alfred Z. Spector

Readings in Object-Oriented Database Systems
Edited by Stanley B. Zdonik and David Maier

The Object Database Standard: ODMG-93

Release 1.2

Edited by
R.G.G. Cattell

With contributions by

Tom Atwood
Douglas Barry
Joshua Duhl
Jeff Eastman
Guy Ferran
David Jordan
Mary Loomis
Drew Wade

Morgan Kaufmann Publishers, Inc.
San Francisco, California

Sponsoring Editor   Michael B. Morgan
Production Manager   Yonie Overton
Production Editor   Cheri Palmer
Editorial Assistant   Jane Elliott
Cover Design   Lori Margulies, based on original cover design by Patty King
Copyeditor   Ken DellaPenta
Printer   Edwards Brothers, Inc.

This book has been author-typeset using FrameMaker.

Morgan Kaufmann Publishers, Inc.
Editorial and Sales Office
340 Pine Street, Sixth Floor
San Francisco, CA 94104-3205
USA
Telephone   415 / 392-2665
Facsimile   415 / 982-2665
Internet   mkp@mkp.com

Library of Congress Cataloging-in-Publication Data is available for this book.
ISBN 1-55860-396-4

Contents

Preface

This book is intended for programmers, end-users, managers, students, and researchers interested in a standard for object database management systems. The ODMG-93 standard described in this book is the result of many years of work, with contributions from many companies. Implementations of ODMG-93 will be available in 1995, so this book should be useful in development, research, teaching, and better understanding the database industry.

This reprint contains changes that are in Release 1.2 of ODMG-93. It reflects various corrections and improvements to Release 1.1 of the specification. Given our extensive discussions and implementations of ODMG-93 to date, we expect this release to be stable; it is our intent that future releases be backward-compatible with Release 1.2. There are a number of features we have deferred to future work; we have already begun work on Release 2.0 at the time of this writing. Since ODMG is not a formal standards body, it has no means for direct distribution of this document. We are publishing the specification as a book to make it easily accessible.

Important changes have been made to most of the chapters in the book. Chapter 2 has been rewritten to improve readability. Significant SQL-92 compatibility enhancements have been added to the Object Query Language in Chapter 4. More rigorous specifications and improvements have been made throughout the document, particularly in Chapters 5 and 6. We have taken advantage of the fact that the Release 1.1 printing sold out to allow us to distribute a number of edits and clarifications based on our experience with the standard and its implementation.

If you want the latest information on the status of the ODMG standards proposal (in order to find out when and how future releases will be available), or if you have corrections or suggestions, please see the ODMG contact information on page 10.

Thanks are due to many people for helping in this endeavor; these contributors are listed in Chapter 1.

Rick Cattell
August 1, 1995

Chapter 1

Overview

1.1 Background

This document describes the results of several years work toward standards for object database management systems (ODBMSs) undertaken by the members of the Object Database Management Group (ODMG). Our proposal represents a substantial creative effort that we believe has significantly changed the object database industry.

We have worked outside of traditional standards bodies for our efforts in order to make quick progress. Standards groups are well suited to incremental changes to a proposal once a good starting point has been established, but it is difficult to perform substantial creative work in such organizations due to their lack of continuity, large membership, and infrequent meetings. It should be noted that relational database standards started with a database model and language implemented by the largest company involved (IBM); for our work, we have picked and combined the best features of half a dozen implementations we had available to us.

1.1.1 Importance of a Standard

Before ODMG, the lack of a standard for object databases was a major limitation to their more widespread use. The success of relational database systems did not result simply from a higher level of data independence and a simpler data model than previous systems. Much of their success came from the standardization that they offer. The acceptance of the SQL standard allows a high degree of portability and interoperability between systems, simplifies learning new relational DBMSs, and represents a wide endorsement of the relational approach.

All of these factors are important for object DBMSs, as well. In fact, these factors are even more important, because most of the products in this area are offered by young companies — portability and endorsement of the approach are essential to a customer. In addition, the scope of object DBMSs is more far-reaching than that of relational DBMSs, integrating the programming language and database system, and encompassing all of an application's operations and data. A standard is critical to making such applications practical.

The intense ODMG effort has given the object database industry a "jump start" toward standards that would otherwise have taken many years. ODMG enables many vendors to support and endorse a common object database interface to which customers write their applications.

1.1.2 Goals

Our primary goal is to put forward a set of standards allowing an ODBMS customer to write portable applications, i.e., applications that could run on more than one ODBMS product. The data schema, programming language binding, and data manipulation and query languages must be portable. Eventually, we hope our standards proposal will be helpful in allowing interoperability between the ODBMS products, as well, e.g., for heterogeneous distributed databases communicating through the OMG Object Request Broker.

We are striving to bring programming languages and database systems to a new level of integration, moving the industry forward as a whole through the practical impetus of real products that conform to a more comprehensive standard than is possible with relational systems. We have gone further than the least common denominator of the first relational standards, and we want to provide portability for the entire application, not just the small portion of the semantics encoded in embedded SQL statements.

The ODMG member companies, representing almost the entire ODBMS industry, are supporting this standard. Thus, our proposal has become a de facto standard for this industry. We also plan to submit our proposal to standards groups for further endorsement.

We do not wish to produce identical ODBMS products. Our goal is source code portability; there is a lot of room for future innovation in a number of areas. There will be differences between products in performance, languages supported, functionality unique to particular market segments (e.g., version and configuration management), accompanying programming environments, application construction tools, small versus large scale, multithreading, networking, platform availability, depth of functionality, suites of predefined type libraries, GUI builders, design tools, and so on.

Wherever possible, we have used existing work as the basis for our proposals, from standards groups and from the literature. But, primarily, our work is derived by combining the strongest features of the ODBMS products currently available. These products offer demonstrated implementations of our standards components that have been tried in the field.

1.1.3 Definition

It is important to define the scope of our efforts, since ODBMSs provide an architecture that is significantly different than other DBMSs — they are a revolutionary rather than an evolutionary development. Rather than providing only a high-level language such as SQL for data manipulation, an ODBMS transparently integrates database capability with the application programming language. This transparency makes it unnecessary to learn a separate DML, obviates the need to explicitly copy and translate data between database and programming language representations, and supports substantial performance advantages through data caching in applications. The ODBMS includes the query language capability of relational systems as well, and the query language model is more powerful; e.g., it incorporates lists, arrays, and results of any type.

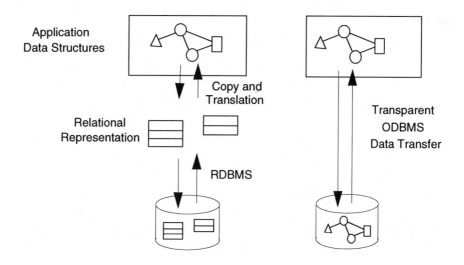

Figure 1-1. Comparison of DBMS Architectures

In summary, we define an *ODBMS* to be a DBMS that integrates database capabilities with object-oriented programming language capabilities. An ODBMS makes database objects appear as programming language objects, in one or more existing programming languages. The ODBMS extends the language with transparently persistent data, concurrency control, data recovery, associative queries, and other database capabilities. For more extensive definition and discussion of ODBMSs, the reader is referred to textbooks in this area (e.g., Cattell, *Object Data Management*).

In contrast to extended relational database systems, ODBMSs require standards based on integration with existing programming language syntax, semantics, and compilers. ODBMSs have been integrated with C++, C, Smalltalk, and LISP. There is some overlap with extended relational database systems, since we want our query language to retain some compatibility with the evolving SQL standard. However, the object paradigm must incorporate the entire application, not just embedded database statements, to be truly beneficial.

1.2 Architecture

In order to understand the chapters of this book, it is necessary to understand the overall architecture of ODBMSs.

1.2.1 Major Components

The major components of ODMG-93 are described in subsequent chapters of the book:

> *Object Model.* The common data model to be supported by ODBMSs is described in Chapter 2. We have used the OMG Object Model as the basis for our model. The OMG core model was designed to be a common denominator for object request brokers, object database systems, object programming languages, and other applications. In keeping with the OMG Architecture, we have designed an ODBMS *profile* for their model, adding components (e.g., relationships) to the OMG core object model to support our needs.

> *Object Definition Language.* The data definition language for ODBMSs is described in Chapter 3. We call this the object definition language, or ODL, to distinguish it from traditional database data definition languages, or DDLs. We use the OMG interface definition language (IDL) as the basis for ODL syntax.

> *Object Query Language.* We define a declarative (nonprocedural) language for querying and updating database objects. This object query language, or OQL, is described in Chapter 4. We have used the relational standard SQL as the basis for OQL, where possible, though OQL supports more powerful capabilities. We hope that SQL3 will converge with OQL at a future date.

> *C++ Language Binding.* Chapter 5 presents the standard binding of ODBMSs to C++; it explains how to write portable C++ code that manipulates persistent objects. This is called the C++ OML, or object manipulation language. The C++ binding also includes a version of the ODL that uses C++ syntax, a mechanism to invoke OQL, and procedures for operations on databases and transactions.

> *Smalltalk Language Binding.* Chapter 6 presents the standard binding of ODBMSs to Smalltalk; it defines the binding in terms of the mapping between ODL and Smalltalk, which is based on the OMG Smalltalk binding for IDL. The Smalltalk binding also includes a mechanism to invoke OQL, and procedures for operations on databases and transactions.

It is possible to read and write the same database from both Smalltalk and C++, as long as the programmer stays within the common subset of supported data types. More chapters may be added at a future date for other language bindings. Note that unlike SQL in relational systems, ODBMS data manipulation languages are tailored to specific application programming languages, in order to provide a single, integrated environment for programming and data manipulation. We don't believe exclusively in a universal DML syntax. We go further than relational systems, as we support a unified object model for sharing data across programming languages, as well as a common query language.

1.2.2 Additional Components

In addition to the object database standards, ODMG has produced some ancillary results aimed at forwarding the ODBMS industry. These have been included as appendices:

> *OMG Object Model Profile.* Appendix A describes the differences between our object model and the OMG object model, so that Chapter 2 can stand alone. As just mentioned, we have defined the components in an ODBMS profile for OMG's model. This appendix delineates these components.

> *OMG ORB Binding.* Appendix B describes how ODBMS objects could participate as OMG objects, through an adaptor to an object request broker (ORB) that routes object invocations through object identifiers provided by an ODBMS. We also outline the reverse: how ODBMSs can make use of the OMG ORB.

1.2.3 ODBMS Architecture Perspective

A better understanding of the architecture of an ODBMS will help put the components we have discussed into perspective.

Figure 1-2 illustrates the use of the typical ODBMS product that we are trying to standardize. The programmer writes declarations for the application schema (both data and interfaces) plus a source program for the application implementation. The source program is written in a programming language (PL) such as C++, using a class library that provides full database OML including transactions and object query. The schema declarations may be written in an extension of the programming language syntax, labeled PL ODL in the figure, or in a programming language-independent ODL. The latter could be used as a higher-level design language, or to allow schema definition independent of programming language.

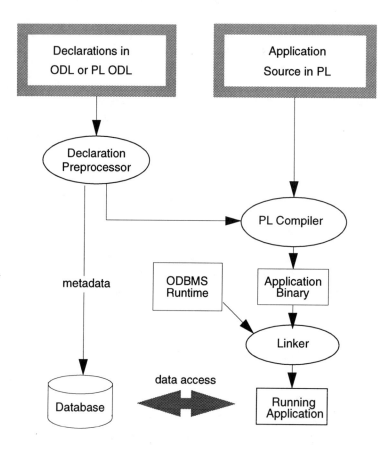

Figure 1-2. Using an ODBMS

The declarations and source program are then compiled and linked with the ODBMS to produce the running application. The application accesses a new or existing database, whose types must conform to the declarations. Databases may be shared with other applications on a network; the ODBMS provides a shared service for transaction and lock management, allowing data to be cached in the application.

1.3 Status

This document describes Release 1.2 of the ODMG-93 standard. The ODMG voting member companies and many of the reviewer member companies are committed to support this standard in their products by the end of 1995.

1.3.1 Participants

As of August 1995, the participants in the ODMG are

- Rick Cattell (ODMG chair, object model workgroup chair, Release 1.0 editor), SunSoft
- Jacob Stein (ODMG vice-chair), reviewer member, Sybase
- Douglas Barry (ODMG executive director, Release 1.1 & 1.2 editor), Barry & Associates
- Jeff Eastman (Smalltalk editor), Windward Solutions
- David Jordan (C++ editor), AT&T Bell Laboratories
- Mary Loomis (staff), Hewlett-Packard (formerly Versant)
- Tom Atwood, Ken Sinclair, voting member, Object Design
- Francois Bancilhon, Guy Ferran, Sophie Gamerman, voting member, O_2 Technology
- Dirk Bartels (C++ workgroup chair), voting member, POET Software
- Adam Springer (Smalltalk workgroup chair), voting member, GemStone Systems
- Henry Strickland, Steve Zhang, voting member, Versant Object Technology
- Drew Wade, Jacob Butcher, Dann Treachler, voting member, Objectivity
- Rafiul Ahad, reviewer member, Hewlett-Packard
- Jurgen Annevelink, reviewer member, Fujitsu Open Systems Solutions
- Mark Berler, reviewer member, American Management Systems
- Jean-Claude Franchitti, reviewer member, Unidata
- Marc Gille, reviewer member, MICRAM Object Technology
- William Herndon, reviewer member, MITRE Corporation
- Richard Jensen, reviewer member, Persistence Software
- Andre Pruitt, reviewer member, Lockheed Martin
- Paul Richards, reviewer member, Electronic Data Systems
- Shirley Schneider, Paul Martel, reviewer member, ONTOS
- Jamie Shiers, reviewer member, CERN
- John Shiner, reviewer member, Andersen Consulting
- Robert Roffe, reviewer member, ADB
- David Wells, reviewer member, Texas Instruments

It is to the personal credit of all the authors and other participants that the ODMG standard has been produced and revised expeditiously. The original author/editors were Tom Atwood, Rick Cattell, Joshua Duhl, Guy Ferran, Mary Loomis, and Drew Wade. The current author/editors are Douglas Barry, Rick Cattell, Jeff Eastman, David Jordan, and Mary Loomis. Dirk Bartels, Adam Springer, and Rick Cattell served as working group chairs for chapter specifications. All of the contributors put substantial time and personal investment into the meetings and this document. They showed remarkable dedication to our goals; no one attempted to twist the process to his or her company's advantage. The reviewers were also very helpful, always ready to contribute. Given that we had no starting point from which to work, we could have taken years to develop and agree upon any one of the chapters in this book, yet the group moved quickly to all the results reported here.

ODMG working group members not listed above have contributed to the past and present content of this document. Thanks are due to Phil Gust and Bill Wilkinson. Many of the photos were taken by Jacob Stein.

In addition to the regular ODMG participants above, we received valuable feedback from others in academia and industry. We would like to thank our academic reviewers, Dave Maier, Dave Dewitt, Mike Carey, Eliot Moss, Marv Solomon, and Stan Zdonik, for their thoughtful and prompt feedback. We would also like to thank industry reviewers José Blakely, Brian Keefe, Frank Manola, and Richard Steiger for their help.

1.3.2 History

Some of the history and methodology of ODMG may be helpful in understanding our work and the philosophy behind it. We learned a lot about how to make quick progress in standards in a new industry while avoiding "design by committee."

ODMG was conceived at the invitation of Rick Cattell in the summer of 1991, in an impromptu breakfast with ODBMS vendors frustrated at the lack of progress toward ODBMS standards. Our first meeting was at SunSoft in the fall of 1991, and we released a press announcement outlining our intent in December.

The group adopted rules that have been instrumental to our quick progress. We wanted to remain small and focused. Five original voting members turned out to be ideal — the right size for good discussion, and a small, odd number for timely voting. We admitted members as individuals, not as companies; substitute representatives from member companies would have required constant rehashing of old issues. Our membership requirements were strict: members had to devote one week per month to ODMG work, they had to be senior technical experts in the field, and their companies had to commercially ship an object database meeting the definition in this chapter. Members temporarily lost voting privileges if they missed meetings and lost their membership altogether if they repeatedly missed deliverables or meetings.

The members have met intensely — averaging about two days a month — to maintain our continuity and focused energy. We devised a reviewer membership to allow other contributors to provide input without bogging down the regular meetings with many people. We found dedicated expert volunteers to serve as author/editors for the chapters. The chair maintained a schedule and regularly hassled members in an attempt to keep deliverables on time. In short, we were serious about making this effort a success.

1.3.3 Accomplishments

Since the publication of Release 1.0, a number of activities have occurred.

1. Incorporation of the ODMG and the establishment of an office.

2. Affiliation with the Object Management Group (OMG), OMG adoption (February 1994) of a Persistence Service endorsing ODMG-93 as a standard interface for storing persistent state, and OMG adoption (May 1995) of a Query Service endorsing the ODMG OQL for querying OMG objects.

3. Establishment of liaisons with ANSI X3H2 (SQL), X3J16 (C++), and X3J20 (Smalltalk), and several ad hoc meetings between ODMG and X3H2 for converging OQL and SQL3.

4. Re-definition of reviewer membership to allow the user community to participate more fully in the efforts of the ODMG.

5. Publication of several articles written by ODMG participants that explain the goals of the ODMG and how they will affect the industry.

6. Collection of feedback on Release 1.0 and 1.1, of which much was used in this release.

1.3.4 Next Steps

We now plan to proceed with several actions in parallel to keep things moving quickly.

1. Distribute Release 1.2 through this book.

2. Complete implementation of the specifications in our respective products.

3. Collect feedback and corrections for the next release of our standards specification.

4. Continue to maintain and develop our work.

5. Continue to submit our work to OMG or ANSI groups, as appropriate.

1.3.5 Suggestion and Proposal Process

If you have suggestions for improvements in future versions of our document, we welcome your input. We recommend that change proposals be submitted as follows:

1. State the essence of your proposal.

2. Outline the motivation and any pros/cons for the change.

3. State exactly what edits should be made to the text, referring to page number, section number, and paragraph.

4. Send your proposal to proposal@odmg.org.

1.3.6 Contact Information

For more information about the ODMG and the latest status of its work, send electronic mail to info@odmg.org. You will receive an automated response.

If you have questions on ODMG-93, send them to question@odmg.org.

If you have additional questions, or if you want membership information for the ODMG, please contact ODMG's executive director, Douglas Barry, at dbarry@odmg.org, or contact:

> Object Database Management Group
> 13504 Clinton Place
> Burnsville, MN 55337 USA
> voice: +1-612-953-7250
> fax: +1-612-397-7146
> web: http://www.odmg.org/

1.3.7 Related Standards

There are references in this book to ANSI X3 documents, including SQL specifications (X3H2), Object Information Management (X3H7), the X3/SPARC/DBSSG OODB Task Group Report (contact fong@ecs.ncsl.nist.gov), and the C++ standard (X3J16). ANSI documents can be obtained from:

> X3 Secretariat, CBEMA
> 1250 Eye Street, NW, Suite 200
> Washington, DC 20005-3922 USA

There are also references to Object Management Group (OMG) specifications, from the Object Request Broker (ORB) Task Force (also called CORBA), the Object Model Task Force (OMTF), and the Object Services Task Force (OSTF). OMG can be contacted at:

> Object Management Group
> Framingham Corporate Center
> 492 Old Connecticut Path
> Framingham, MA 01701 USA
> voice: +1-508-820-4300
> fax: +1-508-820-4303
> email: omg@omg.org
> web: http://www.omg.org/

Chapter 2

Object Model

2.1 Overview

This chapter defines the Object Model supported by ODMG-compliant object database management systems. The Object Model is important because it specifies the kinds of semantics that can be defined explicitly to an ODBMS. Among other things, the semantics of the Object Model determine the characteristics of objects, how objects can be related to each other, and how objects can be named and identified.

Chapter 3 defines a programming-language independent Object Definition Language (ODL), to be used to specify application object models. ODL syntax is presented for all of the constructs explained in this chapter for the Object Model. It is also used in this chapter to define the operations on the various objects of the object model. Chapters 5 and 6, respectively, define the C++ and Smalltalk programming language bindings for ODL and for manipulating objects. Programming languages have some inherent semantic differences; these are reflected in the ODL bindings. Thus some of the constructs that appear here as part of the Object Model may be modified slightly by the binding to a particular programming language. These differences are explained in the chapter about the particular binding.

The Object Model specifies the constructs that are supported by an ODBMS:

- The basic modeling primitives are the *object* and the *literal*. Each object has a unique identifier. A literal has no identifier.
- The state of an object is defined by the values it carries for a set of *properties*. These properties can be *attributes* of the object itself or *relationships* between the object and one or more other objects. Typically the values of an object's properties can change over time.
- The behavior of an object is defined by the set of *operations* that can be executed on or by the object. For example, a Document object includes a format operation.
- Objects and literals can be categorized by their *types*. All elements of a given type have a common range of states (i.e., the same set of properties) and common behavior (i.e., the same set of defined operations). An object is sometimes referred to as an *instance* of its type.
- A *database* stores objects, enabling them to be shared by multiple users and applications. A database is based on a *schema* that is defined in ODL and contains instances of the types defined by its schema.

The ODMG Object Model specifies what is meant by objects, literals, types, operations, properties, attributes, relationships, and so forth. An application developer uses the constructs of the ODMG Object Model to construct the object model for the application. The application's object model specifies particular types, such as Document, Author, Publisher, and Chapter, and the operations and properties of each of these types. The application's object model is the database's (logical) schema.

Analogous to the ODMG Object Model for object databases is the relational model for relational databases, as embodied in SQL. The relational model is the fundamental definition of a relational database management system's functionality. The ODMG Object Model is the fundamental definition of an ODBMS's functionality. The ODMG Object Model includes significantly richer semantics than does the relational model, by declaring relationships and operations explicitly.

2.2 Types and Classes; Interfaces and Implementations

There are two aspects to the definition of a type. A type has an *interface* specification and one or more *implementation* specifications. The interface defines the external characteristics of the objects of the type. These external characteristics are the objects' aspects that are visible to users of the objects. These are the operations that can be invoked on the objects and the state variables whose values can be accessed. By contrast, a type's implementation defines the internal aspects of the objects of the type.

An implementation of a type consists of a *representation* and a set of *methods*. The representation is a data structure. The methods are procedure bodies. There is a method for each of the operations defined in the type's interface specification. A method implements the externally visible behavior of its associated operation. A method might read or modify the representation of an object's state or invoke operations defined on other objects. There can also be methods and data structures in an implementation that have no direct counterpart operations or state variables in the type interface. The internals of an implementation are not visible to the users of the objects.

The distinction between interface and implementation is important. The separation between these two is the way that the Object Model reflects encapsulation. The ODL of Chapter 3 is used to specify the interfaces of types in application object models. Chapters 5 and 6, respectively, define the C++ and Smalltalk constructs used to specify the implementations of these types.

A type can have more than one implementation specification, although only one implementation can be used in any particular program. For example, a type could have one C++ implementation and another Smalltalk implementation. Or a type could have one C++ implementation for one machine architecture, and another C++ implementation for a different machine architecture. Separating the interface from the implementations keeps the semantics of the type from becoming tangled with representation details.

Separating the interface from the implementations is a positive step toward multi-lingual access to objects of a single type and sharing of objects across heterogeneous computing environments.

We sometimes loosely refer to an interface by itself as a type, and to an implementation of a type as a *class*. An object is an instance of a class. A class specification, then, is used to implement all instances of the type. For example, a C++ class specification is used by both a C++ compiler and an ODBMS to create instances (objects) of the type.

2.2.1   Subtyping and Inheritance

Like many object models, the ODMG Object Model includes inheritance-based type-subtype relationships. These relationships are commonly represented in graphs; each node is a type and each arc connects one type, called the *supertype*, and another type, called the *subtype*. The type/subtype relationship is sometimes called an *is-a* relationship, or simply an *ISA* relationship. It is also sometimes called a *generalization-specialization* relationship. The supertype is the more general type; the subtype is the more specialized.

```
interface Employee {...};
interface Professor : Employee {...};
interface Associate_Professor : Professor {...};
```

For example, Associate_Professor is a subtype of Professor; Professor is a subtype of Employee. An instance of the subtype is also logically an instance of the supertype. Thus an Associate_Professor instance is also logically a Professor instance. That is, Associate_Professor is a special case of Professor.

An object's *most specific type* is the type that describes all the behavior and properties of the instance. For example, the most specific type for an Associate_Professor object is the Associate_Professor interface; that object also carries type information from the Professor and Employee interfaces. An Associate_Professor instance conforms to all the behaviors defined in the Associate_Professor interface, the Professor interface, and any supertypes of the Professor interface (and their supertypes, ...). Where an object of type Professor can be used, an object of type Associate_Professor can be used instead, because Associate_Professor inherits from Professor.

A subtype's interface may define characteristics in addition to those defined on its supertypes. These new aspects of state or behavior apply only to instances of the subtype (and any of its subtypes). A subtype's interface also can be refined to specialize state and behavior. For example, the Employee type might have an operation for calculate_ paycheck. The Salaried_Employee and Hourly_Employee subtypes might each refine that behavior to reflect their specialized needs. The polymorphic nature of object programming would then enable the appropriate behavior to be invoked at runtime, dependent on the actual type of the instance.

```
interface Teaching_Assistant : Employee, Student {...};
```

The ODMG Object Model supports multiple inheritance. Therefore it is possible that a type inherits characteristics that have the same name, but different semantics, from two different supertypes. The model currently does not specify how name clashes are resolved; this is implementation-defined.

```
interface Salaried_Employee : Employee {...};
interface Hourly_Employee : Employee {...};
```

Some types are directly instantiable and are called *concrete types*. Others are called *abstract types* and cannot be directly instantiated. For example, if it is logically the case that all employees are either hourly or salaried, then Salaried_Employee and Hourly_Employee would be concrete types, and their supertype Employee would be an abstract type. There could be no direct instantiations of Employee. ODL does not explicitly denote whether a type is abstract or concrete.

2.2.2 Extents

The *extent* of a type is the set of all instances of the type within a particular database. If an object is an instance of type **A**, then it will of necessity be a member of the extent of **A**. If type **A** is a subtype of type **B**, then the extent of **A** is a subset of the extent of **B**.

A relational DBMS maintains an extent for every defined table. By contrast, the object database designer can decide whether the ODBMS should automatically maintain the extent of each type. Extent maintenance includes inserting newly created instances in the set and removing instances from the set as they are deleted. It may also mean creating and managing indexes to speed access to particular instances in the extent. Index maintenance can introduce significant overhead, so the object model definer specifies that the extent should be indexed separately from specifying that the extent should be maintained by the ODBMS.

2.2.3 Keys

In some cases the individual instances of a type can be uniquely identified by the values they carry for some property or set of properties. These identifying properties are called *keys*. In the relational model, these properties (actually, just attributes in relational databases) are called *candidate keys*. A *simple key* consists of a single property. A *compound key* consists of a set of properties. The scope of uniqueness is the extent of the type, thus a type must have an extent to have a key.

2.3 Objects

This section considers each of the following aspects of objects:

- Identifiers, which are used by an ODBMS to distinguish one object from another and to find objects.

- Names, which are designated by programmers or end-users as convenient ways to refer to particular objects.
- Lifetimes, which determine how the memory and storage allocated to objects are managed.
- Structure, which can be either atomic or not, in which case the object is comprised of other objects.

All objects have the following ODL interface, which is implicitly inherited by the definitions of all user-defined objects:

```
interface Object {
    boolean    same_as(in Object anObject);
    Object     copy();
    void       delete();
};
```

2.3.1   Object Identifiers

Because all objects have identifiers, an object can always be distinguished from all other objects within its *storage domain*. In this release of the ODMG Object Model, a storage domain is a database. All identifiers of objects in a database are unique, relative to each other. The representation of the identity of an object is referred to as its *object identifier* (or Object_Id). An object retains the same object identifier for its entire lifetime. Thus the value of an object's identifier will never change. The object remains the same object, even if its attribute values or relationships change. An object identifier is commonly used as a means for one object to reference another.

Note that the notion of object identifier is different from the notion of primary key in the relational model. A row in a relational table is uniquely identified by the value of the column(s) comprising the table's primary key. If the value in one of those columns changes, the row changes its identity and becomes a different row. Even traceability to the prior value of the primary key is lost.

Literals do not have their own identifiers and cannot stand alone as objects; they are embedded in objects and cannot be individually referenced. Literal values are sometimes described as being constant. An earlier release of the ODMG Object Model described literals as being immutable. The value of a literal cannot change. Examples of literal values are the numbers 7 and 3.141596, the characters A and B, and the strings Fred and April 1. By contrast, objects, which have identifiers, have been described as being *mutable*. Changing the values of the attributes of an object, or the relationships in which it participates, does not change the identity of the object.

Object identifiers are generated by the ODBMS, not by applications. There are many possible ways to implement object identifiers. The structure of the bit pattern representing an object identifier is not defined by the Object Model, as this is considered to be an implementation issue, inappropriate for incorporation in the Object Model. Instead, the operation same_as() is supported which allows the identity of any two objects to be compared.

2.3.2   Object Names

In addition to being assigned an object identifier by the ODBMS, an object may be given one or more names that are meaningful to the programmer or end-user. The ODBMS provides a function that it uses to map from an object name to an object identifier. The application can refer at its convenience to an object by name; the ODBMS applies the mapping function to determine the object identifier that locates the desired object. ODMG expects names to be commonly used by applications to refer to "root" objects, which provide entry points into databases.

Object names are like global variable names in programming languages. They are not the same as keys. A key is comprised of properties specified in an object type's interface. An object name, by contrast, is not defined in a type interface and does not correspond to an object's property values.

The scope of uniqueness of names is a database. The Object Model does not include a notion of hierarchical name spaces within a database, or of name spaces that span databases.

2.3.3   Object Lifetimes

The *lifetime* of an object determines how the memory and storage allocated to the object are managed. The lifetime of an object is specified at the time the object is created.

Two lifetimes are supported in the Object Model:

- **transient**
- **persistent**

An object whose lifetime is transient is allocated memory that is managed by the programming language run-time system. Sometimes a transient object is declared in the heading of a procedure and is allocated memory from the stack frame created by the programming language run-time system when the procedure is invoked. That memory is released when the procedure returns. Other transient objects are scoped by a process rather than a procedure activation and are typically allocated to either static memory or the heap by the programming language system. When the process terminates, the memory is deallocated. An object whose lifetime is persistent is allocated memory and storage managed by the ODBMS run-time system. These objects continue to exist after the procedure or process that creates them terminates. Persistent objects are sometimes referred to as *database objects*. Particular programming languages may refine the notion of transient lifetimes in manners consistent with their lifetime concepts.

An important aspect of object lifetimes is that they are independent of types. A type may have some instances that are persistent and others that are transient. This independence of type and lifetime is quite different from the relational model. In the relational model, any type known to the DBMS by definition has only persistent instances, and any type not known to the DBMS (i.e., any type not defined using SQL) by definition has only transient instances. Because the ODMG Object Model supports independence of type and lifetime, both persistent and transient objects can be manipulated using the same operations. In the relational model, SQL must be used for defining and using persistent data, while the programming language is used for defining and using transient data.

2.3.4 Atomic Objects

An atomic object type is user-defined. There are no built-in atomic object types included in the ODMG Object Model. See Section 2.5 for information about the properties and behavior that can be defined for atomic objects.

2.3.5 Collection Objects

In the ODMG Object Model, object types that are not atomic are collections. Instances of these types comprise distinct elements, each of which can be an instance of an atomic type, another collection, or a literal type. Literal types will be discussed in section 2.4. An important distinguishing characteristic of a collection is that *all* the elements of the collection must be of the *same* type. They are either all the same atomic type, or all the same type of collection, or all the same type of literal.

The collection types supported by the ODMG Object Model include

- **Set<t>**
- **Bag<t>**
- **List<t>**
- **Array<t>**

Each of these is a type generator, parameterized by the type shown within the angle brackets. All the elements of a Set object are of the same type **t.** All the elements of a List object are of the same type **t.** In the following interfaces, we have chosen to use the ODL type any to represent these typed parameters, recognizing that this can imply a heterogeneity which is not the intent of this object model.

Collections all have the following operations:

```
interface Collection : Object {
    unsigned long cardinality();
    boolean      is_empty();
    void         insert_element(in any element);
    void         remove_element(in any element);
    boolean      contains_element(in any element);
    Iterator     create_iterator();
};
```

```
interface Iterator : Object {
    exception     Empty();
    exception     NoMoreElements();
    boolean       not_done();
    boolean       next(out any next_obj);
    void          advance() raises(NoMoreElements);
    any           get_element() raises(Empty);
    void          reset();
};
```

An element can be inserted into a collection or can be removed from a collection. A collection object can be tested for the existence of a particular element. An Iterator, which is a mechanism for accessing the elements of a collection object, can be created. A copy of a collection returns a new collection object whose elements are the same as the elements of the original collection object. This is a shallow copy operation.

2.3.5.1 Set Objects

A Set object is an unordered collection of elements, with no duplicates allowed. Set refines the following operations inherited from its Collection supertype:

```
interface Set : Collection {
    Set           union_with(in Set other);
    Set           intersection_with(in Set other);
    Set           difference_with(in Set other);
    boolean       is_subset_of(in Set other_set);
    boolean       is_proper_subset_of(in Set other_set);
    boolean       is_superset_of(in Set other_set);
    boolean       is_proper_superset_of(in Set other_set);
};
```

The inherited insert_element operation inserts the object passed as its argument into an existing set object. If the object passed as an argument is already a member of the set object, the operation raises an exception. Equality is determined by the element's same_as operator.

In addition to the operations inherited from its supertype, the Set type interface has the conventional mathematical set operations, as well as subsetting and supersetting boolean tests. The union_with, intersection_with, and difference_with operations each returns a new result set object.

2.3.5.2 Bag Objects

A Bag object is an unordered collection of elements that may contain duplicates. Equality of elements is determined by the element's same_as operator. Bag refines the following operations inherited from its Collection supertype: insert_element, remove_element.

The insert_element operation inserts into the bag object the element passed as an argument. If the element is already a member of the bag, it is inserted another time, increasing its multiplicity in the bag.

In addition to the operations inherited from its Collection supertype, the Bag type has the following operations defined in its interface:

```
interface Bag : Collection {
    Bag       union_with(in Bag other);
    Bag       intersection_with(in Bag other);
    Bag       difference_with(in Bag other);
};
```

The union_with operation is equivalent to creating a new bag object that is a copy of the receiver bag, then iterating through the argument's bag and performing an insert into the new bag for each element in that argument bag.

2.3.5.3 List Objects

List object is an ordered collection of elements. In addition to the operations it inherits from its supertype Collection, the List type has these operations specified:

```
interface List : Collection {
    void    replace_element_at(in unsigned long index, in any element);
    any     remove_element_at(in unsigned long index);
    any     retrieve_element_at(in unsigned long index);
    void    insert_element_after(in any obj, in unsigned long index);
    void    insert_element_before(in any obj, in unsigned long index);
    void    insert_element_first (in any obj);
    void    insert_element_last (in any obj);
    any     remove_first_element();
    any     remove_last_element();
    any     retrieve_first_element();
    any     retrieve_last_element();
    List    concat(in List other);
    void    append(in List other);
};
```

These operations are positional in nature, either in reference to a given index or to the beginning or end of a List object. Indexing of a List object starts at 0 (zero).

2.3.5.4 Array Objects

An Array object is a collection with a fixed number of elements that can be located by position. The Array type defines the following operations in addition to those inherited from its supertype Collection:

```
interface Array : Collection {
    void    replace_element_at(in unsigned long index, in any element);
    any     remove_element_at(in unsigned long index);
    any     retrieve_element_at(in unsigned long index);
    void    resize(in unsigned long new_size);
};
```

The remove_element_at operation replaces any current element contained in the cell of the array object identified by position with a null value. It does not remove the cell or change the size of the array. This is in contrast to the remove_element_at operation defined on type List, which does change the number of elements in a List object. The resize operation enables an Array object to change the maximum number of elements it can contain.

2.4 Literals

Literals do not have object identifiers. The Object Model supports three literal types:

- **atomic literal**
- **collection literal**
- **structured literal**

2.4.1 Atomic Literals

Numbers and characters are examples of atomic literal types. Instances of these types are not explicitly created by applications, but rather implicitly exist. The ODMG Object Model supports the following types of atomic literals:

- **Long**
- **Short**
- **Unsigned long**
- **Unsigned short**
- **Float**
- **Double**
- **Boolean**
- **Octet**
- **Char (character)**
- **String**
- **Enum (enumeration)**

These types are all also supported by the OMG Interface Definition Language (IDL). The intent of the Object Model is that a programming language binding should support the language-specific analog of these types, as well as any other atomic literal types defined by the programming language. If the programming language does not contain an analog for one of the Object Model types, then a class library defining the implementation of the type should be supplied as part of the programming language binding.

Enum is a type generator. An Enum declaration defines a named literal type that can take on only the values listed in the declaration. For example, an attribute gender might be defined by

```
attribute Enum gender {male, female};
```

An attribute state_code might be defined by

> attribute Enum state_code {AK,AL,AR,AZ,CA, ... WY};

2.4.2 Collection Literals

The ODMG Object Model supports collection literals of the following types:

- **Set<t>**
- **Bag<t>**
- **List<t>**
- **Array<t>**

These type generators are analogous to those of collection objects, but these collections do not have object identifiers. Their elements, however, can be of literal types or object types.

2.4.3 Structured Literals

A structured literal, or simply *structure*, has a fixed number of elements, each of which has a variable name and can contain either a literal value or an object. An element of a structure is typically referred to by a variable name, e.g., address.zip_code = 12345; address.city = "San Francisco". Structure types supported by the ODMG Object Model include

- **Date**
- **Interval**
- **Time**
- **Timestamp**

These types are defined as in the ANSI SQL specification by the following interfaces:

2.4.3.1 Date

The following interface defines the operations on Date objects.

```
interface Date : Object {
    typedef    unsigned short    ushort;
    enum       Weekday {Sunday, Monday, Tuesday, Wednesday,
                        Thursday, Friday, Saturday};
    enum       Month {January, February, March, April, May, June, July,
                      August, September, October, November, December};

    // used to represent a Date object by a typed value
    struct asValue {ushort month, day, year;};

    ushort     year();
    ushort     month();
    ushort     day();
    ushort     day_of_year();
```

```
    Month      month_of_year();
    Weekday    day_of_week();

    boolean    is_leap_year();
    boolean    is_equal(in Date a_date);
    boolean    is_greater(in Date a_date);
    boolean    is_greater_or_equal(in Date a_date);
    boolean    is_less(in Date a_date);
    boolean    is_less_or_equal(in Date a_date);
    boolean    is_between(in Date a_date, in Date b_date);

    Date       next(in Weekday day);
    Date       previous(in Weekday day);
    Date       add_days(in ushort days);
    Date       subtract_days(in ushort days);
    long       subtract_date(in Date a_date);
};
```

2.4.3.2 Interval

Intervals represent a duration of time and are used to perform some operations on Time and TimeStamp objects.

```
interface Interval : Object {
    typedef    unsigned short     ushort;
    ushort     day();
    ushort     hour();
    ushort     minute();
    float      second();

    // used to represent an Interval object as a typed value
    struct     asValue {ushort day, hour, minute; float second;};

    boolean    is_zero();

    Interval   plus(in Interval an_interval);
    Interval   minus(in Interval an_interval);
    Interval   product(in short val);
    Interval   quotient(in short val);

    boolean    is_equal(in Interval an_interval);
    boolean    is_greater(in Interval an_interval);
    boolean    is_greater_or_equal(in Interval an_interval);
    boolean    is_less(in Interval an_interval);
    boolean    is_less_or_equal(in Interval an_interval);
};
```

2.4.3.3 Time

Times denote specific world times.

```
interface Time : Object {
    typedef short        Time_Zone;

    const   Time_Zone  GMT = 0;
    const   Time_Zone  GMT1 = 1;
    const   Time_Zone  GMT2 = 2;
```

```
        const  Time_Zone  GMT3 = 3;
        const  Time_Zone  GMT4 = 4;
        const  Time_Zone  GMT5 = 5;
        const  Time_Zone  GMT6 = 6;
        const  Time_Zone  GMT7 = 7;
        const  Time_Zone  GMT8 = 8;
        const  Time_Zone  GMT9 = 9;
        const  Time_Zone  GMT10 = 10;
        const  Time_Zone  GMT11 = 11;
        const  Time_Zone  GMT12 = 12;
        const  Time_Zone  GMT_1 = -1;
        const  Time_Zone  GMT_2 = -2;
        const  Time_Zone  GMT_3 = -3;
        const  Time_Zone  GMT_4 = -4;
        const  Time_Zone  GMT_5 = -5;
        const  Time_Zone  GMT_6 = -6;
        const  Time_Zone  GMT_7 = -7;
        const  Time_Zone  GMT_8 = -8;
        const  Time_Zone  GMT_9 = -9;
        const  Time_Zone  GMT_10 = -10;
        const  Time_Zone  GMT_11 = -11;
        const  Time_Zone  GMT_12 = -12;
        const  Time_Zone  USeastern = -5;
        const  Time_Zone  UScentral = -6;
        const  Time_Zone  USmountain = -7;
        const  Time_Zone  USpacific = -8;

        ushort      hour();
        ushort      minute();
        float       second();
        short       tz_hour();
        short       tz_minute();

        boolean     is_equal(in Time a_Time);
        boolean     is_greater(in Time a_Time);
        boolean     is_greater_or_equal(in Time a_Time);
        boolean     is_less(in Time a_Time);
        boolean     is_less_or_equal(in Time a_Time);
        boolean     is_between(in Time a_Time,
                              in Time b_Time);

        Time        add_interval(in Interval an_interval);
        Time        subtract_interval(in Interval an_interval);
        Interval    subtract_time(in Time a_time);
};
```

2.4.3.4 TimeStamp

TimeStamps consist of an encapsulated Date and Time.

```
interface TimeStamp : Object {
    typedef    unsigned short    ushort;
    Date                the_date();
    Time                the_time();
```

```
ushort          year();
ushort          month();
ushort          day();
ushort          hour();
ushort          minute();
float           second();
short           tz_hour();
short           tz_minute();

TimeStamp       plus(in Interval an_interval);
TimeStamp       minus(in Interval an_interval);

boolean         is_equal(in TimeStamp a_Stamp);
boolean         is_greater(in TimeStamp a_Stamp);
boolean         is_greater_or_equal(in TimeStamp a_Stamp);
boolean         is_less(in TimeStamp a_Stamp);
boolean         is_less_or_equal(in TimeStamp a_Stamp);
boolean         is_between(in TimeStamp a_Stamp,
                           in TimeStamp b_Stamp);
};
```

2.4.3.5 User-defined Structures

Because the Object Model is extensible, developers can define other structure types as needed. The Object Model includes a built-in type generator Struct, to be used to define application structures. For example:

```
attribute Struct Address {String dorm_name, String room_no} dorm_address;
```

The operations defined by the generator for the structure types include the following:

```
interface Struct {
   unsigned long size();
   void       set_element (in any field, in any value);
   any        get_element(in any field);
   void       clear_element(in any field);
   Struct     copy();
   void       delete();
};
```

Structures may be freely composed. The Object Model supports sets of structures, structures of sets, arrays of structures, and so forth. This composability allows the definition of types like Degrees, as a list whose elements are structures containing three fields:

```
struct Degree {
   string          school_name;
   string          degree_type;
   unsigned short  degree_year;
};
typedef list<Degree>Degrees;
```

Each Degrees instance could have its elements sorted by value of degree_year.

An implementation may bind the Object Model structures and collections to classes that are provided by the programming language. For example, Smalltalk includes its own Collection, Date, Time, and Timestamp classes.

2.5 Modeling State — Properties

A type defines a set of properties through which users can access, and in some cases directly manipulate, the state of instances of the type. Two kinds of properties are defined in the ODMG Object Model: *attribute* and *relationship*. An attribute is of one type. A relationship is defined between two types, each of which must have instances that are referenceable by object identifiers. Thus literal types, because they do not have object identifiers, cannot participate in relationships.

2.5.1 Attributes

The attribute declarations in an interface define the abstract state of a type. For example, the type Person might contain the following attribute declarations:

```
interface Person {
    attribute short age;
    attribute string name;
    attribute enum gender {male, female};
    attribute Address home_address;
    attribute set<Phone_no> phones;
    attribute Department dept;
};
```

A particular instance of Person would have a specific value for each of the defined attributes. The value for the dept attribute above is the object identifier of an instance of Department. An attribute's value is always either a literal or an object identifier.

It is important to note that an attribute is not the same as a data structure. An attribute is abstract, while a data structure is a physical representation. While it is common for attributes to be implemented as data structures, it is sometimes appropriate for an attribute to be implemented as a method. For example, the age attribute might very well be implemented as a method that calculates age from a stored value of the person's date_of_birth and the current date.

In this release of the ODMG Object Model, attributes are not "first class." This means that an attribute itself is not an object and therefore does not have an object identifier. It is not possible to define attributes of attributes or relationships between attributes or subtype-specific operations for attributes.

2.5.2 Relationships

Relationships are defined between types. The ODMG Object Model supports only binary relationships, i.e., relationships between two types. The model does not support n-ary relationships, which involve more than two types. A binary relationship may be one-to-one, one-to-many, or many-to-many, depending on how many instances of each type participate in the relationship. For example, *marriage* is a one-to-one relationship between two instances of type Person. A woman can have a one-to-many *mother of* relationship with many children. Teachers and students typically participate in many-to-many relationships. Relationships in the Object Model are similar to relationships in entity-relationship data modeling.

Relationships in this release of the Object Model are not named and are not "first class." A relationship is not itself an object and does not have an object identifier. A relationship is defined implicitly by declaration of *traversal paths* that enable applications to use the logical connections between the objects participating in the relationship. Traversal paths are declared in pairs, one for each direction of traversal of the binary relationship. For example, a professor *teaches* courses and a course *is taught by* a professor. The teaches traversal path would be defined in the interface declaration for the Professor type. The is_taught_by traversal path would be defined in the interface declaration for the Course type. The fact that these traversal paths both apply to the same relationship is indicated by an inverse clause in both of the traversal path declarations. For example:

```
interface Professor {
    ...
    relationship Set<Course> teaches
        inverse Course::is_taught_by;
    ...
}
```

and

```
interface Course {
    ...
    relationship Professor is_taught_by
        inverse Professor::teaches;
    ...
}
```

The relationship defined by the teaches and is_taught_by traversal paths is a one-to-many relationship between Professor and Course objects. This cardinality is shown in the traversal path declarations. A Professor instance is associated with a set of Course instances via the teaches traversal path. A Course instance is associated with a single Professor instance via the is_taught_by traversal path.

Traversal paths that lead to many objects can be unordered or ordered, as indicated by the type of collection specified in the traversal path declaration. If Set is used, as in Set<Course>, the objects at the end of the traversal path are unordered. If List is used, as in the following definition, the objects at the end of the traversal path are ordered. The order_by clause is applicable only when List is used in declaring the traversal path:

```
interface Professor {
    ...
    relationship List<Course> teaches
        inverse Course::is_taught_by
        {order_by Course::course_no};
    ...
}
```

The ODBMS is responsible for maintaining the referential integrity of relationships. This means that if an object that participates in a relationship is deleted, then any traversal path to that object must also be deleted. For example if a particular Course instance is deleted, then not only is that object's reference to a Professor instance via the is_taught_by traversal path deleted, but also any references in Professor objects to the Course instance via the teaches traversal path must also be deleted. Maintaining referential integrity ensures that applications cannot dereference traversal paths that lead to non-existent objects.

```
attribute Student top_of_class;
```

An attribute may be Object-valued. This kind of attribute enables one object to reference another, without expectation of an inverse traversal path or referential integrity.

It is important to note that a relationship traversal path is not equivalent to a pointer. A pointer in C++ or Smalltalk has no connotation of a corresponding inverse traversal path, which would form a relationship.

The operations defined on relationship parties and their traversal paths vary according to the traversal path's cardinality. When the traversal path has cardinality "one," operations are defined to create a relationship, to destroy a relationship, and to traverse the relationship. When the traversal path has cardinality "many," the traversal path additionally supports all of the behaviors defined above on the Collection class used to define the behavior of the relationship. Traversal paths will guarantee referential integrity in all cases.

2.6 Modeling Behavior — Operations

Besides the attribute and relationship properties, the other characteristic of a type is its behavior, which is specified as a set of *operation signatures*. Each signature defines the name of an operation, the name and type of each of its arguments, the types of value(s) returned, and the names of any *exceptions* (error conditions) the operation can raise. Our Object Model specification for operations is identical to the OMG CORBA specification for operations.

An operation is defined on only a single type. There is no notion in the Object Model of an operation that exists independent of a type, or of an operation defined on two or more types. An operation name need be unique only within a single type definition. Thus different types could have operations defined with the same name. The names of these operations are said to be *overloaded*. When an operation is invoked using an overloaded name, a specific operation must be selected for execution. This selection, sometimes called *operation name resolution* or *operation dispatching*, is based on the most specific type of the object supplied as the first argument of the actual call.

The ODMG had several reasons for choosing to adopt this single-dispatch model rather than a multiple-dispatch model. The major reason was for consistency with the C++ and Smalltalk programming languages. This consistency enables seamless integration of ODBMSs into the object programming environment. Another reason to adopt the classical object model was to avoid incompatibilities with the OMG CORBA object model, which is classical rather than general.

An operation may have side effects. Some operations may return no value. The ODMG Object Model does not include formal specification of the semantics of operations. It is good practice, however, to include comments in interface specifications, for example remarking on the purpose of an operation, any side effects it might have, pre- and post-conditions, and any invariants it is intended to preserve.

The Object Model assumes sequential execution of operations. It does not require support for concurrent or parallel operations, but does not preclude an ODBMS from taking advantage of multiprocessor support.

2.6.1 Exception Model

The ODMG Object Model supports dynamically nested exception handlers, using a termination model of exception handling. Operations can raise exceptions, and exceptions can communicate exception results. Exceptions in the Object Model are themselves objects and have an interface which allows them to be related to other exceptions in a generalization-specialization hierarchy.

A root type Exception is provided by the ODBMS. This type includes an operation to issue a message noting that an unhandled exception of type Exception_type has occurred to terminate the process. Information on the cause of an exception or the context in which it occurred is passed back to the exception handler as properties of the Exception object.

Control is as follows:

1. The programmer declares an exception handler within scope **s** capable of handling exceptions of type **t**.

2. An operation within a contained scope **sn** may "raise" an exception of type **t**.

3. The exception is "caught" by the most immediately containing scope that has an exception handler. The call stack is automatically unwound by the run-time system out to the level of the handler. Destructors are called for all objects allocated in intervening stack frames. Any transactions begun within a nested scope, that is unwound by the run-time system in the process of searching up the stack for an exception handler, are aborted.

4. When control reaches the handler, the handler may either decide that it can handle the exception or pass it on (reraise it) to a containing handler.

An exception handler that declares itself capable of handling exceptions of type **t**, will also handle exceptions of any subtype of **t**. A programmer who requires more specific control over exceptions of a specific subtype of **t** may declare a handler for this more specific subtype within a contained scope.

The signature of an operation includes declaration of the exceptions that the operation can raise.

2.7 Metadata

Metadata is descriptive information about database objects. The metadata defines the schemas of databases; it is used by the ODBMS in structuring databases and at runtime to guide access to databases. Metadata is accessible to tools and applications using the same operations that apply to user-defined types. In the OMG CORBA environment, the metadata are stored in an IDL Interface Repository.

2.7.1 The Full Built-in Type Hierarchy

Figure 2-1 shows the full set of built-in types of the Object Model type hierarchy. Concrete types are shown in non-italic font and are directly instantiable. Abstract types are shown in italics. In the interests of simplifying matters, both types and type generators are included in the same hierarchy. Type generators are signified by angle brackets (e.g., Set<>).

2.7.2 Type Compatibility Rules

The ODMG Object Model is strongly typed. Every object or literal has a type, and every operation requires typed operands. The rules for type identity and type compatibility are defined in this section.

Two objects or literals have the same type if and only if they have been declared to be instances of the same named type. Objects or literals that have been declared to be instances of two different types are not of the same type, even if the types in question define the same set of properties and operations. Type compatibility follows the subtyping relationships defined by the type hierarchy. If **TS** is a subtype of **T**, then an object of type **TS** can be assigned to a variable of type **T**, but the reverse is not possible. No implicit conversions between types are provided by the Object Model.

Two atomic literals have the same type if they belong to the same set of literals. Depending on programming language bindings, implicit conversions may be provided between the scalar literal types, i.e., Long, Short, Unsigned long, Unsigned short, Float, Double, Boolean, Octet, Char. No implicit conversions are provided for structured literals.

Literal_type
   Atomic_literal
        Long
        Short
        Unsigned long
        Unsigned short
        Float
        Double
        Boolean
        Octet
        Char
        String
        Enum<>
   Collection_literal
        Set<>
        Bag<>
        List<>
        Array<>
   Structured_literal
        Date
        Time
        Timestamp
        Interval
        Structure<>
Object_type
   Atomic_object
   Collection
        Set<>
        Bag<>
        List<>
        Array<>

Figure 2-1. Full Set of Built-in Types

2.7.3   Null Value

For every literal type (e.g., float or Set<>) there exists another literal type supporting a null value (e.g., nullable_float or nullable_Set<>). This nullable type is the same as the literal type augmented by the null value "nil". The semantics of null is the same as that defined by SQL-92.

2.7.4   Table Type

In order to make clear that the ODMG data model encompasses the relational data model, the type generator Table<> is defined in the ODMG data model as a synonym of the type generator Bag<Struct<>> such that

    Table(a1:t1, a2:t2, ... , an:tn)

is equivalent to the definition

    Bag<Struct< a1:t1, a2:t2, ... , an:tn>>

2.8 Transaction Model

Programs that use persistent objects are organized into *transactions*. Transaction management is an important ODBMS functionality, fundamental to database integrity, shareability, and recovery. Any access, creation, modification, and deletion of persistent objects must be done within a transaction.

A transaction is a unit of logic for which an ODBMS guarantees atomicity, consistency, isolation, and durability. *Atomicity* means that the transaction either finishes or has no effect at all. *Consistency* means that a transaction takes the database from one internally consistent state to another internally consistent state. There may be times during the transaction when the database is inconsistent. However, no other user of a database sees changes made by a transaction until that transaction commits. Concurrent users always see an internally consistent database. *Isolation* means that the execution of concurrent transactions must yield results which are indistinguishable from results that would have been obtained if the transactions had been executed serially. This property is sometimes called serializability. *Durability* means that the effects of committed transactions are preserved, even if there should be failures of storage media, loss of memory, or system crashes. Once a transaction has committed, the ODBMS guarantees that changes made by that transaction are never lost. When a transaction commits, all of the changes made by that transaction are permanently installed in the database and made visible to other users of the database. When a transaction aborts, none of the changes made by it are installed in the database, including any changes made prior to the time of abort.

In the Object Model, transient objects are not subject to transaction semantics. This means aborting a transaction does not restore the state of modified transient objects.

The Object Model assumes a linear sequence of transactions executing within a single process, running against a single logical database. Note that a single logical database may be implemented as one or more physical databases, possibly distributed in a network. The Object Model neither requires nor precludes support for transactions that span multiple processes or that span more than one logical database.

2.8.1 Locking and Concurrency Control

The ODMG Object Model uses a conventional lock-based approach to concurrency control. Locks can be acquired on particular objects. Some compliant implementations may either force or allow locks to be escalated to some other level of granularity.

The ODMG Object Model supports traditional pessimistic concurrency control as its default policy, but does not preclude DBMSs from supporting a wider range of concurrency control policies. The default model requires acquisition of a read lock on an object before it can be read, and acquisition of a write lock on an object before that object can be modified. Readers of an object do not conflict with other readers, but writers conflict with both readers and writers. If there is a conflict, the DBMS allows the holder of the lock to proceed and the transaction that requested the conflicting lock waits until the holder completes. The holder may complete by either committing or aborting, at which point all its locks are released. Transactions subject to this protocol serialize in commit order.

2.8.2 Transaction Operations

An ODBMS provides a type Transaction with the following operations:

```
interface Transaction {
    void    begin();
    void    commit();
    void    abort();
    void    checkpoint();
};
```

The begin operation starts a Transaction. Transactions must be explicitly created and started; they are not automatically created by the ODBMS when a database is opened or following a transaction commit or abort.

The commit operation causes all persistent objects created or modified during this transaction to become accessible to other transactions running against the database in other processes. The Transaction instance is deleted and all locks held by that Transaction instance are released.

The abort operation causes the Transaction object to be deleted and the database to be returned to the state it was in prior to the beginning of the transaction. All locks held by the transaction are released.

The checkpoint operation writes all modified objects to the database and retains all locks held by the transaction. It does not delete the Transaction object.

2.9 Database Operations

An ODBMS may manage one or more logical databases, each of which may be stored in one or more physical databases. Each logical database is an instance of the type Database, which is supplied by the ODBMS. The type Database supports the following operations:

```
interface Database {
    void            open(in string database_name);
    void            close();
    void            bind(in any an_object, in string name);
    any             lookup(in string object_name);
};
```

The open operation must be invoked, with a database name as its argument, before any access can be made to the persistent objects in the database. The Object Model requires only a single database to be open at a time. Implementations may extend this capability, including transactions that span multiple databases. The close operation must be invoked when a program has completed all access to the database. When the ODBMS closes a database, it performs necessary cleanup operations.

The lookup operation is used to find the identifier of the object with the name supplied as the argument to the operation. This operation is defined on the Database type, because the scope of object names is the database. The names of objects in the database, the names of types in the database schema, and the extents of types instantiated in the database are global to the database. They become accessible to a program once it has opened the database. Named objects are convenient entry points to the database. A name is bound to an object using the bind operation.

The Database type may also support operations designed for database administration, e.g., move, copy, reorganize, verify, backup, restore. These kinds of operations are not specified here, as they are considered an implementation consideration outside the scope of the Object Model.

2.10 Possible Future Revisions

The current ODMG Object Model is intended to be extensible to support additional functionality through successive releases of the ODMG standard. In the interest of achieving a standard we have intentionally restricted the functionality of the Object Model. However, there are many areas of additional functionality we could support. This section outlines the areas we expect to consider in future revisions. This section is included for two reasons: first, to let reviewers of the base model know what functionality has been considered and deferred, and second, to allow implementors to begin developing pilot implementations in some of these areas. These pilots will give us a solid body of implementation experience on which to base our discussions of incorporation of new functionality.

2.10.1 Types, Extents

1. Multiple implementations are visible to the programmer. An implementation may be chosen at object creation time.

2. Indices may be dynamically created and destroyed either by explicit programmer request or by the query processor if indices would be useful.

3. Multiple types may share one implementation.

4. Instance properties may be defined on types, e.g., the color attribute inherited from type Bird is defined to be "red" for birds of subtype Cardinal.

5. Named sub-extents of a type may be defined. If a predicate determining instance membership in a particular sub-extent is specified in the type declaration, then the ODBMS automatically maintains the sub-extent as well as, or in lieu of, the full extent.

2.10.2 Objects

1. An object may be an instance of more than one type.

2. An object may dynamically acquire/lose a type.

3. An object may dynamically change representations (i.e., implementations).

4. An object's lifetime may be changed. The typical use for this is for a transient object to become persistent.

5. Object versions are supported. Configurations containing specific versions of component objects are supported.

6. Versions of types are supported.

7. The type programmer may extend or replace the built-in collection types.

2.10.3 Attributes

1. Attributes may have properties.

2. Attribute types may participate in supertype/subtype relationships with other attribute types.

3. Integrity constraints can be declared on attribute types.

2.10.4 Relationships

1. Relationships become first-class objects.

2. Relationships may have properties, e.g., transitive, reflexive, or other attributes.

3. Relationship types may participate in supertype/subtype relationships with other relationship types.

4. The consists_of relationship is supported, with predefined delete, move, copy ... semantics.

5. An object may acquire attribute values by virtue of its participation in a relationship, e.g., Course.enrollment defines the number of students enrolled in a course, Student.course_load defines the number of courses a student is currently taking.

6. The type definer may supply an implementation for a relationship type rather than using one of the built-in implementations.

2.10.5 Operations

1. Remote operations are explicitly supported.

2. Parallel operations are explicitly supported.

3. Free-standing operations, not defined on a single type, are supported.

2.10.6 Transactions

1. Long-lived transactions are supported.

2. A single transaction may access objects in more than one database (distributed transactions and XA protocol).

3. More than one process may participate in a single transaction.

4. Transaction consistency applies to transient as well as persistent objects.

5. Nested transactions are supported.

2.10.7 Databases

1. Versions of database schemas are supported.

2. Subschemas are supported.

3. Versions of subschemas are supported.

4. Access control and security considerations are supported.

5. Type definitions are treated as objects.

6. Metadata is exposed as a predefined schema.

7. Hierarchical name spaces are supported.

Chapter 3

Object Definition Language

3.1 Introduction

The Object Definition Language (ODL) is a specification language used to define the interfaces to object types that conform to the ODMG Object Model. The primary objective of the ODL is to facilitate portability of database schemas across conforming ODBMSs. ODL also provides a step toward interoperability of ODBMSs from multiple vendors.

Several principles have guided the development of the ODL, including

- ODL should support all semantic constructs of the ODMG Object Model.
- ODL should not be a full programming language, but rather a specification language for interface signatures.
- ODL should be programming-language independent.
- ODL should be compatible with the OMG's Interface Definition Language (IDL).
- ODL should be extensible, not only for future functionality, but also for physical optimizations.
- ODL should be practical, providing value to application developers, while being supportable by the ODBMS vendors within a relatively short time frame after publication of the specification.

ODL is not intended to be a full programming language. It is a specification language for interface signatures. Database management systems (DBMSs) have traditionally provided interfaces that support data definition (using a Data Definition Language — DDL) and data manipulation (using a Data Manipulation Language — DML). The DDL allows users to define their data types and interfaces. DML allows programs to create, delete, read, change, etc., instances of those data types. The ODL described in this chapter is a DDL for object types. It defines the characteristics of types, including their properties and operations. ODL defines only the signatures of operations and does not address definition of the methods that implement those operations. ODMG-93 does not provide a standard OML. Chapters 5 and 6 define standard APIs to bind conformant ODBMSs to C++ and to Smalltalk.

The ODL is intended to define object types that can be implemented in a variety of programming languages. Therefore ODL is not tied to the syntax of a particular programming language; users can use ODL to define schema semantics in a programming-language independent way. A schema specified in ODL can be supported by any ODMG-compliant ODBMS and by mixed-language implementations. This portability is necessary for an application to be able to run with minimal modification on a variety of ODBMSs. Some applications may in fact need simultaneous support from multiple ODBMSs. Others may need to access objects created and stored using different programming languages. ODL provides a degree of insulation for applications against the variations in both programming languages and underlying ODBMS products.

The C++ ODL and Smalltalk ODL bindings defined in Chapters 5 and 6 respectively are designed to fit smoothly into the declarative syntax of their host programming language. Due to the differences inherent in the object models native to these programming languages, it is not always possible to achieve consistent semantics across the programming-language specific versions of ODL. Our goal has been to minimize these inconsistencies, and we have noted in Chapters 5 and 6 the restrictions applicable to each particular language binding.

The syntax of ODL extends IDL —the Interface Definition Language developed by the OMG as part of the Common Object Request Broker Architecture (CORBA). IDL was itself influenced by C++, giving ODL a C++ flavor. Appendix B, "ODBMS in the OMG ORB Environment," describes the relationship between ODL and IDL. ODL adds to IDL the constructs required to specify the complete semantics of the ODMG Object Model.

ODL also provides a context for integrating schemas from multiple sources and applications. These source schemas may have been defined with any number of object models and data definition languages; ODL is a sort of lingua franca for integration. For example, various standards organizations like STEP/PDES (EXPRESS), ANSI X3H2 (SQL), ANSI X3H7 (Object Information Management), CFI (CAD Framework Initiative), and others have developed a variety of object models and, in some cases, data definition languages. Any of these models can be translated to an ODL specification (Figure 3-1). This common basis then allows the various models to be integrated with common semantics. An ODL specification can be realized concretely in an object programming language like C++ or Smalltalk.

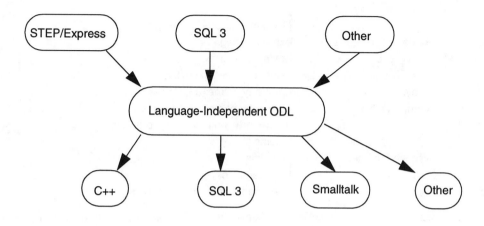

Figure 3-1. ODL Mapping to Other Languages

3.2 Specification

A type is defined by specifying its interface in ODL. The top-level BNF for ODL is as follows:

```
<interface_dcl>        ::=  <interface_header>
                            [ : <persistence_dcl> ] { [ <interface_body> ] } ;
<persistence_dcl>      ::=  persistent | transient
<interface_header>     ::=  interface <identifier>
                            [ <inheritance_spec> ]
                            [ <type_property_list> ]
```

The characteristics of the type itself appear first, followed by lists that define the properties and operations of its interface. Any list may be omitted if it is not applicable in the interface.

3.2.1 Type Characteristics

Supertype information, extent naming, and specification of keys (i.e., uniqueness constraints) are all characteristics of types, but do not apply directly to the types' instances. The BNF for type characteristics follows.

```
<inheritance_spec>     ::=  : <scoped_name> [ , <inheritance_spec> ]
<type_property_list>

                       ::=  ( [ <extent_spec> ] [ <key_spec> ] )
<extent_spec>          ::=  extent <string>
<key_spec>             ::=  key[s] <key_list>
<key_list>             ::=  <key> | <key> , <key_list>
<key>                  ::=  <property_name> | ( <property_list> )
<property_list>        ::=  <property_name>
                            | <property_name> , <property_list>
<property_name>        ::=  <identifier>
<scoped_name>          ::=  <identifier>
                            | :: <identifier>
                            | <scoped_name> :: <identifier>
```

Each supertype must be specified in its own type definition. Each attribute or relationship traversal path named as (part of) a type's key must be specified in the key_spec of the type definition. The extent and key definitions may be omitted if inapplicable to the type being defined. A type definition should include no more than one extent or key definition.

A simple example for the interface definition of a Professor type is

```
interface Professor: Person
(       extent professors
        keys faculty_id, soc_sec_no): persistent
{
        properties
        operations
};
```

Keywords are highlighted.

3.2.2 Instance Properties

A type's instance properties are the attributes and relationships of its instances. These properties are specified in attribute and relationship specifications. The BNF follows.

```
<interface_body>   ::=  <export> | <export> <interface_body>
<export>           ::=   <type_dcl> ;
                         | <const_dcl> ;
                         | <except_dcl> ;
                         | <attr_dcl> ;
                         | <rel_dcl> ;
                         | <op_dcl> ;
```

3.2.2.1 Attributes

The BNF for specifying an attribute follows.

```
<attr_dcl>              ::=  [ readonly ] attribute
                             <domain_type> <attribute_name>
                             [ <fixed_array_size>]
<domain_type>           ::=  <simple_type_spec>
                             | <struct_type>
                             | <enum_type>
```

For example, adding attribute definitions to the Professor type's ODL specification:

```
interface Professor: Person
(          extent professors
           keys faculty_id, soc_sec_no): persistent
{
           attribute String name;
           attribute Unsigned Short faculty_id[6];
           attribute Long soc_sec_no[10] ;
           attribute Address address;
           attribute Set<string> degrees;
           relationships
           operations
};
```

Note that the keyword attribute is mandatory.

3.2.2.2 Relationships

A relationship specification names and defines a traversal path for a relationship. A traversal path definition includes designation of the target type, ordering information, and information about the inverse traversal path found in the target type. The BNF for relationship specification follows.

```
<rel_dcl>               ::=  relationship
                             <target_of_path> <identifier>
                             [ inverse <inverse_traversal_path> ]
                             [ { order_by <attribute_list> } ]
<target_of_path>        ::=  <identifier>
                             | <rel_collection_type> < <identifier> >
<inverse_traversal_path>
                        ::=  <identifier> :: <identifier>
<attribute_list>        ::=  <scoped_name>
                             | <scoped_name> , <attribute_list>
```

Traversal path cardinality information is included in the specification of the target of a traversal path. The target type must be specified with its own type definition, unless the relationship is recursive. Use of the collection_type option of the BNF indicates cardinality greater than one on the target side. If this option is omitted, the cardinality on the target side is one. The most commonly used collection types are expected to be Set, for unordered members on the target side of a traversal path, and List, for ordered members on the target side. Bags are supported as well. An ordering criterion is specified with the order_by clause. Each attribute used in an ordering criterion must be defined in the attribute list of the target type's definition. The inverse traversal path must be defined in the property list of the target type's definition. If an inverse traversal path is not specified, the relationship is considered to be unidirectional. For example, adding relationships to the Professor type's interface specification:

```
interface Professor: Person
(        extent professors
         keys faculty_id, soc_sec_no): persistent
{
         attribute String name;
         attribute Unsigned Short faculty_id[6];
         attribute Long soc_sec_no[10] ;
         attribute Address address;
         attribute Set<string> degrees;
         relationship Set<Student> advises inverse Student::advisor;
         relationship Set<TA> teaching_assistants inverse TA::works_for;
         relationship Department department
                 inverse Department::faculty;
         operations
};
```

The keyword relationship is mandatory.

Note that the attribute and relationship specifications can be mixed in the property list. It is not necessary to define all of one kind of property, then all of the other kind.

3.2.3 Operations

ODL is compatible with IDL for specification of operations. The high-level BNF for operations follows.

```
<op_dcl>              ::=  [ oneway ] <op_type_spec> <identifier>
                           <parameter_dcls> [<raises_expr>]
                           [<context_expr>]
<op_type_spec>        ::=  <simple_type_spec>
                           | void
<parameter_dcls>      ::=  ( [ <param_dcl_list> ] )
<param_dcl_list>      ::=  <param_dcl>
                           | <param_dcl> , <param_dcl_list>
```

<param_dcl>	::=	<param_attribute><simple_type_spec><declarator>
<param_attribute>	::=	**in** | **out**| **inout**
<raises_expr>	::=	**raises (** <scoped_name_list>**)**
<context_expr>	::=	**context (** <string_literal_list> **)**
<scoped_name_list>	::=	<scoped_name>
		| <scoped_name> **,** <scoped_name_list>
<string_literal_list>	::=	<string_literal>
		| <string_literal> **,** <string_literal_list>

See Section 3.5 for the full BNF for operation specification.

3.3 An Example in ODL

This section illustrates the use of ODL to declare the schema for a sample application based on a university database. The object types in the sample application are shown as rectangles in Figure 3-2. Relationship types are shown as lines. The cardinality permitted by the relationship type is indicated by the arrows on the ends of the lines:

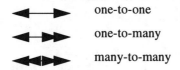

one-to-one

one-to-many

many-to-many

In the example, the type Professor is a subtype of the type Employee, and the type TA (for Teaching Assistant) is a subtype of both Employee and Student. Large gray arrows run from subtype to supertype in the figure.

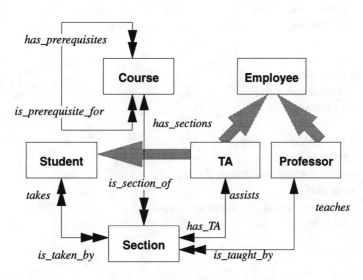

Figure 3-2. Graphical Representation of Schema

An ODL definition for the interfaces of the schema's types follows:

```
interface Course
(       extent courses
        keys name, number)
{
        attribute String name;
        attribute String number;
        relationship List<Section> has_sections
            inverse Section::is_section_of
            {order_by Section::number};
        relationship Set<Course> has_prerequisites
            inverse Course::is_prerequisite_for;
        relationship Set<Course> is_prerequisite_for
            inverse Course::has_prerequisites;

        Boolean offer (in Unsigned Short semester) raises (already_offered);
        Boolean drop (in Unsigned Short semester) raises (not_offered);
};
interface Section
(       extent sections
        key (is_section_of, number))
{
        attribute String number;
        relationship Professor is_taught_by inverse Professor::teaches;
        relationship TA has_TA inverse TA::assists;
        relationship Course is_section_of inverse Course::has_sections;
        relationship Set<Student> is_taken_by inverse Student::takes;
};

interface Employee
(       extent employees
        key (name, id))
{
        attribute String name;
        attribute Short id;
        attribute Unsigned Short annual_salary;
        void hire ();
        void fire () raises (no_such_employee);
};
```

```
interface Professor: Employee
(       extent professors)
{
        attribute Enum Rank {full, associate, assistant} rank;
        relationship Set<Section> teaches inverse Section::is_taught_by;
        Short grant_tenure () raises (ineligible_for_tenure);
};

interface TA: Employee, Student
()
{
        relationship Section assists inverse Section::has_TA;
};

interface Student
(       extent students
        keys name, student_id)
{
        attribute String name;
        attribute String student_id;
        attribute Struct Address {String college, String room_number}
            dorm_address;
        relationship Set<Section> takes inverse Section::is_taken_by;
        Boolean register_for_course (in Unsigned Short course,
            in Unsigned Short Section)
            raises (unsatisfied_prerequisites, section_full, course_full);
        void drop_course (in Unsigned Short Course)
            raises (not_registered_for_that_course);
        void assign_major (in Unsigned Short Department);
        Short transfer (in Unsigned Short old_section,
            in Unsigned Short new_section)
            raises (section_full, not_registered_in_section);
};
```

3.4 Another Example

Following is another example that will be used as an illustration of ODL. The same example will be used in Chapter 5 to illustrate the binding of ODL to C++. The application manages personnel records. The database manages information about people, their marriages, children, and history of residences. Person has an extent named people. A Person has name, address, spouse, children, and parents properties. The operations birth, marriage, ancestors, and move are also characteristics of Person: birth adds a new child to the children list of a Person instance, marriage defines a spouse for a Person instance, ancestors computes the set of Person instances who are the ancestors of a particular Person instance, and move changes a Person instance's address. An Address is a structure whose properties are number, street, and city_name; number is of type Unsigned Short, street and city are of type String. City has properties city_code, name, and population. City_code is of type Unsigned Short; name is of type String; population is a set of Refs to Person objects. Spouse is a traversal path to a spouse:spouse 1:1 recursive relationship; children is one of the traversal paths of a children:parents m:n recursive relationship. The children of a given Person instance are ordered by birth_date. Parents is the other traversal path of the children:parents relationship.

The ODL specifying the interfaces for this schema follows.

```
interface Person
(      extent people)
{
       attribute String name;
       attribute Struct Address {Unsigned Short number, String street,
           String city_name} address;
       relationship Person spouse inverse Person::spouse;
       relationship Set<Person> children inverse Person::parents
           {order_by birth_date} ;
       relationship List<Person> parents inverse Person::children;
       void birth (in String name);
       Boolean marriage (in String person_name) raises (no_such_person);
       Unsigned Short ancestors (out Set<Person> all_ancestors)
           raises (no_such_person);
       void move (in String new_address);
};


interface City
(      extent cities
       key city_code)
{
       attribute Unsigned Short city_code;
       attribute String name;
       attribute Set<Person> population;
};
```

3.5 ODL Grammar

Following is the complete BNF for the ODL, which includes the IDL. The numbers on the production rules match their numbers in the OMG CORBA specification. Modified production rules have numbers suffixed by an asterisk, e.g., (5*). New production rules have alpha extensions, e.g., (5a).

(1)	<specification> ::= <definition>
	I <definition> <specification>
(2)	<definition>::= <type_dcl> ;
	I <const_dcl> ;
	I <except_dcl> ;
	I <interface> ;
	I <module> ;
(3)	<module>::= **module** <identifier> { <specification> }
(4)	<interface>::= <interface_dcl>
	I <forward_dcl>
(5*)	<interface_dcl>::= <interface_header>
	[: <persistence_dcl>] { [<interface_body>] }
(5a)	<persistence_dcl>::= **persistent** I **transient**
(6)	<forward_dcl>::= **interface** <identifier>
(7*)	<interface_header>::= **interface** <identifier>
	[<inheritance_spec>]
	[<type_property_list>]
(7a)	<type_property_list>
	::= ([<extent_spec>] [<key_spec>])
(7b)	<extent_spec>::= **extent** <string>
(7c)	<key_spec>::= **key[s]** <key_list>
(7d)	<key_list>::= <key> I <key> , <key_list>
(7e)	<key>::= <property_name> I (<property_list>)
(7f)	<property_list>::= <property_name>
	I <property_name> , <property_list>
(7g)	<property_name>::= <identifier>
(8)	<interface_body>::=
	<export> I <export> <interface_body>
(9*)	<export>::= <type_dcl>;
	I <const_dcl>;
	I <except_dcl>;
	I <attr_dcl>;
	I <rel_dcl>;
	I <op_dcl>;
(10)	<inheritance_spec>::=
	: <scoped_name> [, <inheritance_spec>]

(11)   <scoped_name>::= <identifier>
                          | :: <identifier>
                          | <scoped_name> :: <identifier>
(12)   <const_dcl>::= **const** <const_type> <identifier> **=**
                          <const_exp>
(13)   <const_type>::= <integer_type>
                          | <char_type>
                          | <boolean_type>
                          | <floating_pt_type>
                          | <string_type>
                          | <scoped_name>
(14)   <const_exp>::= <or_expr>
(15)   <or_expr>::= <xor_expr>
                          | <or_expr> | <xor_expr>
(16)   <xor_expr>::= <and_expr>
                          | <xor_expr> ^ <and_expr>
(17)   <and_expr>::= <shift_expr>
                          | <and_expr> **&** <shift_expr>
(18)   <shift_expr>::= <add_expr>
                          | <shift_expr> >> <add_exp>
                          | <shift_expr> << <add_expr>
(19)   <add_expr>::= <mult_expr>
                          | <add_expr> **+** <mult_expr>
                          | <add_expr> **-** <mult_expr>
(20)   <mult_expr>::= <unary_expr>
                          | <mult_expr> * <unary_expr>
                          | <mult_expr> **/** <unary_expr>
                          | <mult_expr> **%** <unary_expr>
(21)   <unary_expr>::= <unary_operator> <primary_expr>
                          | <primary_expr>
(22)   <unary_operator>::= **-**
                          | **+**
                          | ~
(23)   <primary_expr>::= <scoped_name>
                          | <literal>
                          | **(** <const_exp> **)**
(24)   <literal>::= <integer_literal>
                          | <string_literal>
                          | <character_literal>
                          | <floating_pt_literal>
                          | <boolean_literal>
(25)   <boolean_literal>::= **TRUE**
                          | **FALSE**

(26)	<positive_int_const>::= <const_exp>
(27)	<type_dcl>::= **typedef** <type_declarator>
	| <struct_type>
	| <union_type>
	| <enum_type>
(28)	<type_declarator>::= <type_spec> <declarators>
(29)	<type_spec>::= <simple_type_spec>
	| <constr_type_spec>
(30)	<simple_type_spec>::= <base_type_spec>
	| <template_type_spec>
	| <scoped_name>
(31)	<base_type_spec>::= <floating_pt_type>
	| <integer_type>
	| <char_type>
	| <boolean_type>
	| <octet_type>
	| <any_type>
(32*)	<template_type_spec>::= <array_type>
	| <string_type>
	| <coll_type>
(32a)	<coll_type> ::= <coll_spec> < <simple_type_spec> >
(32b)	<coll_spec> ::= **Set** | **List** | **Bag**
(33)	<constr_type_spec>::= <struct_type>
	| <union_type>
	| <enum_type>
(34)	<declarators>::= <declarator>
	| <declarator> , <declarators>
(35)	<declarator>::= <simple_declarator>
	| <complex_declarator>
(36)	<simple_declarator>::= <identifier>
(37)	<complex_declarator>::= <array_declarator>
(38)	<floating_pt_type>::= **Float**
	| **Double**
(39)	<integer_type>::= <signed_int>
	| <unsigned_int>
(40)	<signed_int>::= <signed_long_int>
	| <signed_short_int>
(41)	<signed_long_int>::= **Long**
(42)	<signed_short_int>::= **Short**
(43)	<unsigned_int>::= <unsigned_long_int>
	| <unsigned_short_int>
(44)	<unsigned_long_int>::= **Unsigned Long**
(45)	<unsigned_short_int>::= **Unsigned Short**

(46)   <char_type>::= **Char**

(47)   <boolean_type>::= **Boolean**

(48)   <octet_type>::= **Octet**

(49)   <any_type>::= **Any**

(50)   <struct_type>::= **Struct** <identifier> **{** <member_list> **}**

(51)   <member_list>::= <member> | <member>
                    <member_list>

(52)   <member>::= <type_spec> <declarators> ;

(53)   <union_type>::= **union** <identifier> **switch**
                    (<switch_type_spec> **)** **{** <switch_body> **}**

(54)   <switch_type_spec>::= <integer_type>
                    | <char_type>
                    | <boolean_type>
                    | <enum_type>
                    | <scoped_name>

(55)   <switch_body>::= <case> | <case> <switch_body>

(56)   <case>::= <case_label_list> <element_spec> ;

(56a)   <case_label_list>::= <case_label>
                    | <case_label> <case_label_list>

(57)   <case_label>::= **case** <const_exp> **:**
                    | **default :**

(58)   <element_spec>::= <type_spec> <declarator>

(59)   <enum_type>::= **Enum** <identifier> **{** <enumerator_list> **}**

(59a)   <enumerator_list>::= <enumerator>
                    | <enumerator> , <enumerator_list>

(60)   <enumerator>::= <identifier>

(61*)   <array_type>::= <array_spec> **<** <simple_type_spec> **,**
                    <positive_int_const> **>**
                    | <array_spec> **<** <simple_type_spec> **>**

(61a*)   <array_spec>::= **Array** | **Sequence**

(62)   <string_type>::=**String** **<** <positive_int_const> **>**
                    | **String**

(63)   <array_declarator>::= <identifier> <array_size_list>

(63a)   <array_size_list>::= <fixed_array_size>
                    | <fixed_array_size> <array_size_list>

(64)   <fixed_array_size>::= **[** <positive_int_const> **]**

(65*)   <attr_dcl> ::= **[readonly] attribute**
                    <domain_type> <attribute_name>
                    [<fixed_array_size> **]**

(65a)   <domain_type>::= <simple_type_spec>
                    | <struct_type>
                    | <enum_type>

(65b)	<rel_dcl> ::= **relationship**
	<target_of_path>
	<identifier>
	inverse <inverse_traversal_path>
	[{ **order_by** <attribute_list> }]
(65c)	<target_of_path>::= <identifier>
		<rel_collection_type> < <identifier> >
(65d)	<inverse_traversal_path>::=
	<identifier> **::** <identifier>
(65e)	<attribute_list>::= <scoped_name>
		<scoped_name> , <attribute_list>
(65f)	<rel_collection_type::= **Set**	**List**	**Bag**	**Array**
(66)	<except_dcl>::= **exception** <identifier>
	{ [<member_list>] }
(67)	op_dcl>::= [<op_attribute>] <op_type_spec>
	<identifier> <parameter_dcls>
	[<raises_expr>] [<context_expr>]
(68)	<op_attribute>::= **oneway**
(69)	<op_type_spec>::= <simple_type_spec>
		void
(70)	<parameter_dcls>::= ([<param_dcl_list>])
(70a)	<param_dcl_list>::= <param_dcl>
		<param_dcl> , <param_dcl_list>
(71)	<param_dcl>::= <param_attribute> <simple_type_spec>
	<declarator>
(72)	<param_attribute>::= **in**
		out
		inout
(73)	<raises_expr>::= **raises** (<scoped_name_list>)
(73a)	<scoped_name_list>::= <scoped_name>
		<scoped_name> ,
	<scoped_name_list>
(74)	<context_expr>::= **context** (<string_literal_list>)
(74a)	<string_literal_list>::= <string_literal>
		<string_literal> , <string_literal_list>

Chapter 4

Object Query Language

4.1 Introduction

In this chapter, we describe an object query language named OQL, which supports the ODMG data model. It is complete and simple. It deals with complex objects without privileging the set construct and the select-from-where clause.

We first describe the design principles of the language in Section 4.2, then we introduce in the next sections the main features of OQL. We explain the input and result of a query in Section 4.3. Section 4.4 deals with object identity. Section 4.5 presents the path expressions. In Section 4.6, we show how OQL can invoke operations and Section 4.7 describes how polymorphism is managed by OQL. Section 4.8 concludes this part of the presentation of the main concepts by exemplifying the property of operators composition.

Finally, a formal and complete definition of the language is given in Section 4.9. For each feature of the language, we give the syntax, its semantics, and an example. Alternate syntax for some features are described in Section 4.10, which completes OQL in order to accept any syntactical form of SQL. The chapter ends with the formal syntax, which is given in Section 4.11.

4.2 Principles

Our design is based on the following principles and assumptions:

- OQL relies on the ODMG object model.
- OQL is a superset of the part of standard SQL that deals with database queries. Thus, any *select* SQL sentence which runs on relational tables, works with the same syntax and semantics on collections of ODMG objects. Extensions concern object-oriented notions, like complex objects, object identity, path expression, polymorphism, operation invocation, late binding, etc.
- OQL provides high-level primitives to deal with sets of objects but is not restricted to this collection construct. It also provides primitives to deal with structures, lists, arrays, and treats such constructs with the same efficiency.
- OQL is a functional language where operators can freely be composed, as long as the operands respect the type system. This is a consequence of the fact that the result of any query has a type which belongs to the ODMG type model, and thus can be queried again.

- OQL is not computationally complete. It is a simple-to-use query language which provides easy access to an ODBMS.
- Based on the same type system, OQL can be invoked from within programming languages for which an ODMG binding is defined. Conversely, OQL can invoke operations programmed in these languages.
- OQL does not provide explicit update operators but rather invokes operations defined on objects for that purpose, and thus does not breach the semantics of an ODBMS which, by definition, is managed by the "methods" defined on the objects.
- OQL provides declarative access to objects. Thus OQL queries can be easily optimized by virtue of this declarative nature.
- The formal semantics of OQL can easily be defined.

4.3 Query Input and Result

As a stand-alone language, OQL allows querying denotable objects starting from their names, which act as entry points into a database. A name may denote any kind of object, i.e., atomic, structure, collection, or literal.

As an embedded language, OQL allows querying denotable objects which are supported by the native language through expressions yielding atoms, structures, collections, and literals. An OQL query is a function which delivers an object whose type may be inferred from the operator contributing to the query expression. This point is illustrated with two short examples.

The schema defines the types Person and Employee. These types have the extents Persons and Employees respectively. One of these persons is the chairman (and there is an entry-point Chairman to that person). The type Person defines the name, birthdate, and salary as attributes and the operation age. The type Employee, a subtype of Person, defines the relationship subordinates and the operation seniority.

```
select distinct  x.age
from Persons x
where x.name = "Pat"
```

This selects the set of ages of all persons named Pat, returning a literal of type set<integer>.

```
select distinct struct(a: x.age, s: x.sex)
from Persons x
where x.name = "Pat"
```

This does about the same, but for each person, it builds a structure containing age and sex. It returns a literal of type set<struct>.

    select distinct struct(name: x.name, hps: (select y
                                from x.subordinates as y
                                where y.salary >100000))
    from Employees x

This is the same type of example, but now we use a more complex function. For each employee we build a structure with the name of the employee and the set of the employee's highly paid subordinates. Notice we have used a select-from-where clause in the select part. For each employee x, to compute hps, we traverse the relationship subordinates and select among this set the employees with a salary superior to $100,000. The result of this query is therefore a literal of the type set<struct>, namely:

    set<struct (name: string, hps: bag<Employee>)>

We could also use a select operator in the from part:

    select struct (a: x.age, s: x.sex)
    from(select y from y in Employees where y.seniority ="10") as x
    where x.name = "Pat"

Of course, you do not always have to use a select-from-where clause:

    Chairman

retrieves the Chairman object.

    Chairman.subordinates

retrieves the set of subordinates of the Chairman.

    Persons

gives the set of all persons.

4.4 Dealing with Object Identity

The query language supports both types of objects: mutable (i.e., having an OID) and literal (identity = their value), depending on the way these objects are constructed or selected.

4.4.1 Creating Objects

To create an object with identity a type name constructor is used. For instance, to create a Person defined in the previous example, simply write

    Person(name: "Pat", birthdate: "3/28/56" , salary: 100,000)

The parameters in parentheses allow you to initialize certain properties of the object. Those which are not explicitly initialized are given a default value.

You distinguish such a construction from the construction expressions that yield objects without identity. For instance,

> struct (a: 10, b: "Pat")

creates a structure with two valued fields.

If you now return to the example in Section 4.3, instead of computing literals, you can build objects. For example, assuming that these mutable object types are defined:

> type vectint: set<integer>;
> type stat
> attributes
>> a: integer
>> s: char
> end_type;
> type stats: bag<stat>;

you can carry out the following queries:

> vectint(select distinct.age
>> from Persons
>> where name = "Pat")

which returns a mutable object of type **vectint** and

> stats(select stat (a: age, s: sex)
>> from Persons
>> where name = "Pat")

which returns a mutable object of type **stats**.

4.4.2   Selecting Existing Objects

The extraction expressions may return:

- A collection of objects with identity, e.g., select x from Persons x where x.name ="Pat" returns a collection of persons whose name is Pat.
- An object with identity, e.g., element (select x from Persons x where x.passport_number=1234567) returns the person whose passport number is 1234567.
- A collection of literals, e.g., select x.passport_number from Persons x where x.name="Pat" returns a collection of integers giving the passport numbers of people named Pat.
- A literal, e.g., Chairman.salary.

Therefore the result of a query is an object with or without object identity: some objects are generated by the query language interpreter, and others produced from the current database.

4.5 Path Expressions

As explained above, one can enter a database through a named object, but more generally as long as one gets an object (which comes, for instance, from a C++ expression), one needs a way to *navigate* from it and reach the right data one needs. To do this in OQL, we use the "." (or indifferently "->") notation which enables us to go inside complex objects, as well as to follow simple relationships. For example, we have a Person p and we want to know the name of the city where this person's spouse lives.

Example:

> p.spouse.address.city.name

This query starts from a Person, gets his/her spouse, a Person again, goes inside the complex attribute of type Address to get the City object whose name is then accessed.

This example treated 1-1 relationship, let us now look at n-p relationships. Assume we want the names of the children of the person p. We cannot write p.children.name because children is a list of references, so the interpretation of the result of this query would be undefined. Intuitively, the result should be a collection of names, but we need an unambiguous notation to traverse such a multiple relationship and we use the select-from-where clause to handle collections just as in SQL.

Example:

> select c.name
> from p.children c

The result of this query is a value of type Bag<String>. If we want to get a Set, we simply drop duplicates, like in SQL by using the distinct keyword.

Example:

> select distinct c.name
> from p.children c

Now we have a means to navigate from an object to any object following any relationship and entering any complex subvalues of an object. For instance, we want the set of addresses of the children of each Person of the database. We know the collection named Persons contains all the persons of the database. We have now to traverse two collections: Persons and Person::children. Like in SQL, the select-from operator allows us to query more than one collection. These collections then appear in the from part. In OQL, a collection in the from part can be derived from a previous one by following a path which starts from it.

Example:

```
select c.address
from Persons p,
    p.children c
```

This query inspects all children of all persons. Its result is a value whose type is Bag<Address>.

4.5.1   Predicate

Of course, the where clause can be used to define any predicate which then serves to select only the data matching the predicate. For example, we want to restrict the previous result to the people living on Main Street, and having at least two children. Moreover we are only interested in the addresses of the children who do not live in the same city as their parents.

Example:

```
select c.address
from Persons p,
    p.children c
where p.address.street = "Main Street" and
    count(p.children) >= 2 and
    c.address.city != p.address.city
```

4.5.2   Join

In the from clause, collections which are not directly related can also be declared. As in SQL, this allows computation of *joins* between these collections. This example selects the people who bear the name of a flower, assuming there exists a set of all flowers called Flowers.

Example:

```
select p
from Persons p,
    Flowers f
where p.name = f.name
```

4.6 Method Invoking

OQL allows us to call a method with or without parameters anywhere the result type of the method matches the expected type in the query. The notation for calling a method is exactly the same as for accessing an attribute or traversing a relationship, in the case where the method has no parameter. If it has parameters, these are given between parentheses. This flexible syntax frees the user from knowing whether the property is stored (an attribute) or computed (a method, such as **age** in the following example). This example returns the age of the oldest child of the person "Paul".

Example:

```
select max(select c.age from p.children c)
from Persons p,
where p.name = "Paul"
```

Of course, a method can return a complex object or a collection and then its call can be embedded in a complex path expression. For instance, if **oldest_child** is a method defined on the class **Person** which returns an object of class **Person**, the following example computes the set of street names where the oldest children of Parisian people are living.

Example:

```
select p.oldest_child.address.street
from Persons p
where p.lives_in("Paris")
```

Although **oldest_child** is a method we *traverse* it as if it were a relationship. Moreover, **lives_in** is a method with one parameter.

4.7 Polymorphism

A major contribution of object orientation is the possibility of manipulating polymorphic collections, and thanks to the *late binding* mechanism, to carry out generic actions on the elements of these collections. For instance, the set **Persons** contains objects of class **Person**, **Employee**, and **Student**. So far, all the queries against the **Persons** extent dealt with the three possible objects of the collection.

If one wants to restrict a query on a subclass of **Person**, either the schema provides an extent for this subclass which can then be queried directly, or else the superclass extent can be filtered to select only the objects of the subclass, as shown in the *class indicator* example.

A query is an expression whose operators operate on typed operands. A query is correct if the types of operands match those required by the operators. In this sense, OQL is a typed query language. This is a necessary condition for an efficient query optimizer. When a polymorphic collection is filtered (for instance **Persons**), its elements are statically known to be of that class (for instance **Person**). This means that a property of a subclass (attribute or method) cannot be applied to such an element, except in two important cases: late binding to a method or explicit class indication.

4.7.1 Late Binding

Give the activities of each person.

Example:

    select p.activities
    from Persons p

where **activities** is a method which has three incarnations. Depending on the kind of person of the current **p**, the right incarnation is called. If **p** is an Employee, OQL calls the operation **activities** defined on this object, or else if **p** is a Student, OQL calls the operation **activities** defined for Students, or else, **p** is a Person and OQL calls the method **activities** of the type Person.

4.7.2 Class Indicator

To go down the class hierarchy, a user may explicitly declare the class of an object that cannot be inferred statically. The evaluator then has to check at runtime that this object actually belongs to the indicated class (or one of its subclasses). For example, assuming we know that only **Students** spend their time in following a course of study, we can select those **Persons** and get their grade. We explicitly indicate in the query that these **Persons** are in **Student**:

Example:

    select ((Student)p). grade
    from Persons p
    where "course of study" in p.activities

4.8 Operator Composition

OQL is a purely functional language. All operators can be composed freely as long as the type system is respected. This is why the language is so simple and its manual so short. This philosophy is different from SQL, which is an ad-hoc language whose composition rules are not orthogonal. Adopting a complete orthogonality allows OQL to not restrict the power of expression and makes the language easier to learn without losing the SQL syntax for the simplest queries. However, when very specific SQL syntax does not enter in a pure functional category, OQL accepts these SQL peculiarities as possible syntactical variations. This is explained more specifically in Section 4.10.

Among the operators offered by OQL but not yet introduced, we can mention the set operators (union, intersect, except), the universal (for all) and existential quantifiers (exists), the sort and group by operators, and the aggregation operators (count, sum, min, max, and avg).

To illustrate this free composition of operators, let us write a rather complex query. We want to know the name of the street where employees live and have the smallest salary on average, compared to employees living in other streets. We proceed by steps and then do it as one query. We use OQL define instruction to evaluate temporary results.

Example:

1. Build the extent of class Employee (assuming that it is not supported directly by the schema):

    define Employees as
    > select (Employee) p from Persons p
    > where "has a job" in p.activities

2. Group the employees by street and compute the average salary in each street:

    define salary_map as
    > select street, average_salary:avg(select e.salary from partition)
    > from Employees e
    > group by street: e.address.street

    The result is of type Bag<struct(street: string, average_salary:float)>. The group by operator splits the employees into partitions, according to the criterion (the name of the street where this person lives). The select clause computes, in each partition, the average of the salaries of the employees belonging to the partition.

3. Sort this set by salary:

    define sorted_salary_map as
    > select s from salary_map s order by s.average_salary

    The result is now of type List<struct(street: string, average_salary:float)>.

4. Now get the smallest salary (the first in the list) and take the corresponding street name. This is the final result.

    first(sorted_salary_map).street

Example as a single query:

    first(select street, average_salary: avg(select e.salary from partition)
        from (select (Employee) p from Persons p
            where "has a job" in p.activities) as e
        group by street : e.address.street
        order by average_salary).street

4.9 Language Definition

OQL is an expression language. A query expression is built from typed operands composed recursively by operators. We will use the term *expression* to designate a valid query in this section.

The examples are based on the schema described in Chapter 3.

4.9.1 Queries

A query consists of a (possibly empty) set of query definition expressions followed by an expression, which is evaluated as the query itself. The set of query definition expressions is nonrecursive (although a query may call an operation which issues a query recursively).

Example:

> define jones as select distinct x from Students x where x.name = "Jones";
> select distinct student_id from jones

This defines the set jones of students named Jones and gets the set of their student_ids.

4.9.2 Named Query Definition

If q is a query name and e is a query expression, then define q as e is a query definition expression which defines the query with name q.

Example:

> define Does as select x from Student x where x.name ="Doe"

This statement defines Does as a query returning a bag containing all the students whose name is Doe.

> define Doe as element(select x from Student x where x.name="Doe")

This statement defines Doe as a query which returns the student whose name is Doe (if there is only one, otherwise an exception is raised).

4.9.3 Elementary Expressions

4.9.3.1 Atomic Literals

If l is an atomic literal, then l is an expression whose value is the literal itself. Literals have the usual syntax:

- Object Literal: nil
- Boolean Literal: false, true
- Integer Literal: sequence of digits, e.g, 27
- Float Literal: mantissa/exponent. The exponent is optional, e.g., 3.14 or 314.16e-2
- Character Literal: character between single quotes, e.g., 'z'
- String Literal: character string between double quote, e.g.,"a string"

4.9.3.2 Named Objects

If e is a named object, then e is an expression. It defines the entity attached to the name.

Example:

    Students

This query defines the set of students. We have assumed here that there exists a name Students corresponding to the extent of objects of the class Student.

4.9.3.3 Iterator Variable

If x is a variable declared in a from part of a select-from-where, then x is an expression whose value is the current element of the iteration over the corresponding collection.

4.9.3.4 Named Query

If define q as e is a query definition expression, then q is an expression.

Example:

    Doe

This query returns the student with name Doe. It refers to the query definition expression declared in Section 4.9.2.

4.9.4 Construction Expressions

4.9.4.1 Constructing Objects

If t is a type name, p_1, p_2, ...,p_n are properties of t, and e_1, e_2, ...,e_n are expressions, then t (p_1: e_1..., p_n: e_n) is an expression.

This defines a new object of type t whose properties p_1, p_2, ...,p_n are initialized with the expression e_1, e_2, ...,e_n. The type of e_i must be compatible with the type of p_i.

If t is a type name of a collection and e is a collection literal, then t(e) is a collection object. The type of e must be compatible with t.

Examples:

    Employee (name: "Peter", boss: Chairman)

This creates a mutable Employee object.

    vectint (set(1,3,10))

This creates a mutable set object (see the definition of vectint in Section 4.4.1).

4.9.4.2 Constructing Structures

If $p_1, p_2, ..., p_n$ are property names, and $e_1, e_2, ..., e_n$ are expressions, then struct $(p_1: e_1, p_2: e_2, ..., p_n: e_n)$ is an expression. It defines the structure taking values $e_1, e_2, ..., e_n$ on the properties $p_1, p_2, ..., p_n$.

Note that this dynamically creates an instance of the type struct$(p_1: t_1, p_2: t_2, ..., p_n: t_n)$ if t_i is the type of e_i.

Example:

>   struct(name: "Peter", age: 25);

This returns a structure with two attributes name and age taking respective values Peter and 25.

See also abbreviated syntax for some contexts in Section 4.10.1.

4.9.4.3 Constructing Sets

If $e_1, e_2, ..., e_n$ are expressions, then set$(e_1, e_2, ..., e_n)$ is an expression. It defines the set containing the elements $e_1, e_2, ..., e_n$. It creates a set instance.

Example:

>   set(1,2,3)

This returns a set consisting of the three elements 1,2, and 3.

4.9.4.4 Constructing Lists

If $e_1, e_2, ..., e_n$ are expressions, then list$(e_1, e_2, ..., e_n)$ or simply $(e_1, e_2, ..., e_n)$ are expressions. They define the list having elements $e_1, e_2, ..., e_n$. They create a list instance.

If min, max are two expressions of integer or character types, such that min < max, then list(min .. max) or simply (min .. max) is an expression of value: list(min, min+1, ... max-1, max)

Example:

>   list(1,2,2,3)

This returns a list of four elements.

Example:

>   list(3 .. 5)

This returns the list (3,4,5)

4.9.4.5 Constructing Bags

If e_1, e_2, ..., e_n are expressions, then bag(e_1, e_2, ..., e_n) is an expression. It defines the bag having elements e_1, e_2, ..., e_n. It creates a bag instance.

Example:

    bag(1,1,2,3,3)

This returns a bag of five elements.

4.9.4.6 Constructing Arrays

If e_1, e_2, ..., e_n are expressions, then array(e_1, e_2, ..., e_n) is an expression. It defines an array having elements e_1, e_2, ..., e_n. It creates an array instance.

Example:

    array(3,4,2,1,1)

This returns an array of five elements.

4.9.5   Atomic Type Expressions

4.9.5.1 Unary Expressions

If e is an expression and <op> is a unary operation valid for the type of e, then <op> e is an expression. It defines the result of applying <op> to e.

Arithmetic unary operators: +, -, abs

Boolean unary operator: not

Example:

    not true

This returns false.

4.9.5.2 Binary Expressions

If e_1 and e_2 are expressions and <op> is a binary operation, then e_1<op>e_2 is an expression. It defines the result of applying <op> to e_1 and e_2.

Arithmetic integer binary operators: +, -, *, /, mod (modulo)
Floating point binary operators: +, -, *, /
Relational binary operators: =, !=, <, <=, >, >=

These operators are defined on all atomic types.

Boolean binary operators: and, or

Example:

    count(Students) - count(TA)

This returns the difference between the number of students and the number of TAs.

4.9.5.3 String Expressions

If s_1 and s_2 are expressions of type string, then $s_1 \parallel s_2$, and $s_1 + s_2$ are equivalent expressions of type string whose value is the concatenation of the two strings.

If c is an expression of type character, and s an expression of type string, then c in s is an expression of type boolean whose value is true if the character belongs to the string, else false.

If s is an expression of type string, and i is an expression of type integer, then s[i] is an expression of type character whose value is the $i+1^{th}$ character of the string.

If s is an expression of type string, and low and up are expressions of type integer, then s[low:up] is an expression of type string whose value is the substring of s from the $low+1^{th}$ character up to the $up+1^{th}$ character.

If s is an expression of type string, and pattern a string literal which may include the wildcard characters: "?" or "_", meaning any character, and "*" or "%", meaning any substring including an empty substring, then s like pattern is an expression of type boolean whose value is true if s matches the pattern, else false.

Example:

    'a nice string' like '%nice%str_ng'   is true

4.9.6   Object Expressions

4.9.6.1 Comparison of Mutable Objects

If e_1 and e_2 are expressions which denote mutable objects (objects with identity) of the same type, then $e_1 = e_2$ and $e_1 \mathrel{!=} e_2$ are expressions which return a boolean. The second expression is equivalent to $not(e_1 = e_2)$. Likewise $e_1 = e_2$ is true if they designate the same object.

Example:

    Doe = element(select s from Students s where s.name = "Doe")

is true.

4.9.6.2 Comparison of Immutable Objects

If e_1 and e_2 are expressions which denote immutable objects (literals) of the same type, then $e_1 = e_2$ and $e_1 \mathrel{!=} e_2$ are expressions which return a boolean. The second expression is equivalent to $not(e_1 = e_2)$. Likewise, $e_1 = e_2$ is true if the value e_1 is equal to the value e_2.

4.9.6.3 Extracting an Attribute or Traversing a Relationship from an Object

If e is an expression, if p is a property name, then e->p and e.p are expressions. These are alternate syntax to extract property p of an object e.

If e happens to designate a deleted or a nonexisting object, i.e., nil, an attempt to access the attribute or to traverse the relationship raises an exception. However, a query may test explicitly if an object is different from nil before accessing a property.

Example:

    Doe.name

This returns Doe.

Example:

    Doe->spouse != nil and Doe->spouse->name = "Carol"

This returns true, if Doe has a spouse whose name is Carol, or else false.

4.9.6.4 Applying an Operation to an Object

If e is an expression and f is an operation name, then e->f and e.f are expressions. These are alternate syntax to apply an operation on an object. The value of the expression is the one returned by the operation or else the object nil, if the operation returns nothing.

Example:

    jones->number_of_students

This applies the operation number_of_students to jones.

4.9.6.5 Applying an Operation with Parameters to an Object

If e is an expression, if e_1, e_2, ..., e_n are expressions and f is an operation name, then e->f(e_1, e_2, ..., e_n) and e.f(e_1, e_2, ..., e_n) are expressions that apply operation f with parameters e_1, e_2, ..., e_n to object e. The value of the expression is the one returned by the operation or else the object nil, if the operation returns nothing.

In both cases, if e happens to designate a deleted or a nonexisting object, i.e., nil, an attempt to apply an operation to it raises an exception. However, a query may test explicitly if an object is different from nil before applying an operation.

Example:

> Doe->apply_course("Math", Turing)->number

This query calls the operation apply_course on class Student for the object Doe. It passes two parameters, a string and an object of class Professor. The operation returns an object of type Course and the query returns the number of this course.

4.9.6.6 Dereferencing an Object

If e is an expression which denotes an object with identity (a mutable object), then *e is an expression which delivers the value of the object (a literal). Given two variables of type Person, p1 and p2, the predicate p1 = p2 is true if both variables refer to the same object, while *p1 = *p2 is true if the objects have the same values, even if they are not the same object

4.9.7   Collection Expressions

4.9.7.1 Universal Quantification

If x is a variable name, e_1 and e_2 are expressions, e_1 denotes a collection, and e_2 a predicate, then for all x in e_1: e_2 is an expression. It returns true if all the elements of collection e_1 satisfy e_2 and false otherwise.

Example:

> for all x in Students: x.student_id > 0

This returns true if all the objects in the Students set have a positive value for their student_id attribute. Otherwise it returns false.

4.9.7.2 Existential Quantification

If x is a variable name, if e_1 and e_2 are expressions, e_1 denotes a collection, and e_2 a predicate, then exists x in e_1: e_2 is an expression. It returns true if there is at least one element of collection e_1 that satisfies e_2 and false otherwise.

Example:

> exists x in Doe.takes: x.taught_by.name = "Turing"

This returns true if at least one course Doe takes is taught by someone named Turing.

If e is a collection expression, then exists(e) and unique(e) are expressions which return a boolean value. The first one returns true if there exists at least one element in the collection, while the second one returns true if there exists only one element in the collection.

Note that these operators accept the SQL syntax for nested queries like

select ... from col where exists (select ... from col_1 where predicate)

The nested query returns a bag to which the operator exists is applied. This is of course the task of an optimizer to recognize that it is useless to compute effectively the intermediate bag result.

4.9.7.3 Membership Testing

If e_1 and e_2 are expressions, e_2 is a collection, and e_1 has the type of its elements, then e_1 in e_2 is an expression. It returns true if element e_1 belongs to collection e_2.

Example:

Doe in Does

This returns true.

Doe in TA

This returns true if Doe is a Teaching Assistant.

4.9.7.4 Aggregate Operators

If e is an expression which denotes a collection, if <op> is an operator from {min, max, count, sum, avg}, then <op>(e) is an expression.

Example:

max (select salary from Professors)

This returns the maximum salary of the Professors.

4.9.8 Select From Where

If e, e', e_1, e_2, ..., e_n are expressions which denote collections, and x_1, x_2, ..., x_n are variable names if e' is an expression of type boolean, and if *projection* is an expression or the character *, then

select *projection* from e_1 as x_1, e_2 as x_2 ..., e_n as x_n where e'   and

select distinct *projection* from e_1 as x_1, e_2 as x_2 ..., e_n as x_n where e'

are expressions.

The result of the query is a set for a select distinct or a bag for a select.

If you assume e_1, e_2, ..., e_n are all set and bag expressions, then the result is obtained as follows: take the Cartesian product[1] of the sets e_1, e_2, ..., e_n; filter that product by expression e' (i.e., eliminate from the result all objects that do not satisfy boolean expression e'); apply the *projection* to each one of the elements of this filtered set and get the result. When the result is a set (distinct case) duplicates are automatically eliminated.

The situation where one or more of the collections e_1, e_2, ..., e_n is an indexed collection is a little more complex. The select operator first converts all these collections into bags and applies the previous operation. The result is a set (distinct case) or else a bag. So, in this case, we simply transform each of the e_i's into a bag and apply the previous definition.

4.9.8.1 Projection

Before the projection, the result of the iteration over the *from* variables is of type

bag< struct(x_1: type_of(e_1 elements), ... x_n: type_of(e_n elements)) >

The projection is constructed by an expression which can then refer implicitly to the *current* element of this bag, using the variables x_i. If for e_i neither explicit nor implicit variable is declared, then x_i is given an internal system name (which is not accessible by the query anyway).

By convention, if the projection is simply "*", then the result of the select is the same as the result of the iteration.

If the projection is "distinct *", the result of the select is this bag converted into a set.

In all other cases, the projection is explicitly computed by the given expression.

Example:

```
select couple(student: x.name, professor: z.name)
    from Students as x,
         x.takes as y,
         y.taught_by as z
    where z.rank = "full professor"
```

---

1. The Cartesian product between a set and a bag is defined by first converting the set into a bag, and then get the resulting bag, which is the Cartesian product of the two bags.

This returns a bag of objects of type couple giving student names and the names of the full professors from which they take classes.

Example:

```
select  *
from Students as x,
    x.takes as y,
    y.taught_by as z
where z.rank = "full professor"
```

This returns a bag of structures, giving for each student "object", the section object followed by the student and the full professor "object" teaching in this section:

```
bag< struct(x: Student, y: Section, z: Professor) >
```

4.9.8.2 Iterator Variables

A variable, x_i, declared in the *from* part ranges over the collection e_i and thus has the type of the elements of this collection. Such a variable can be used in any other part of the query to evaluate any other expressions (see the Scope Rules in Section 4.9.15). Syntactical variations are accepted for declaring these variables, exactly as with SQL. The *as* keyword may be omitted. Moreover, the variable itself can be omitted too, and in this case, the name of the collection itself serves as a variable name to range over it.

Example:

```
select couple(student: Students.name, professor: z.name)
from Students,
    Students.takes y,
    y.taught_by z
where z.rank = "full professor"
```

4.9.8.3 Predicate

In a select-from-where query, the *where* clause can be omitted, with the meaning of a true predicate.

4.9.9   Group-by Operator

If *select_query* is a select-from-where query, *partition_attributes* is a structure expression and *predicate* a boolean expression, then

> *select_query* group by *partition_attributes*

is an expression and

> *select_query* group by *partition_attributes* having *predicate*

is an expression.

The Cartesian product visited by the select operator is split into partitions. For each element of the Cartesian product, the partition attributes are evaluated. All elements which match the same values according to the given partition attributes, belong to the same partition. Thus the partitioned set, after the grouping operation, is a set of structures: each structure has the valued properties for this partition (the valued *partition_attributes)*, completed by a property which is conventionally called *partition* and which is the bag of all objects matching this particular valued partition.

If the partition attributes are att_1: e_1, att_2: e_2, ..., att_n: e_n, then the result of the grouping is of type

> set< struct(att_1: type_of(e_1), att_2: type_of(e_2), ..., att_n: type_of(e_n),
>
> partition: bag< type_of(grouped elements) >)>

The type of grouped elements is defined as follows.

If the *from* clause declares the variables v_1 on collection col_1, v_2 on col_2, ..., v_n on col_n, the grouped elements is a structure with one attribute, v_k, for each collection having the type of the elements of the corresponding collection partition:

> bag< struct(v_1: type_of(col_1 elements), ..., v_n: type_of(col_n elements))>

If a collection col_k has no variable declared the corresponding attribute has an internal system name.

This partitioned set may then be filtered by the predicate of a *having* clause. Finally, the result is computed by evaluating the *select* clause for this partitioned and filtered set.

The having clause can thus apply aggregate functions on *partition*; likewise the select clause can refer to *partition* to compute the final result. Both clauses can refer also to the partition attributes.

Example:

```
select  *
from  Employees e
group by low:     salary < 1000,
         medium: salary >= 1000 and salary < 10000,
         high:    salary >= 10000
```

This gives a set of three elements, each of which has a property called *partition* which contains the bag of employees that enter in this category. So the type of the result is

> set<struct(low: boolean, medium: boolean, high: boolean,
>   partition: bag<struct(e: Employee)>)>

The second form enhances the first one with a *having* clause which enables you to filter the result using aggregative functions which operate on each partition.

Example:

```
select  department,
    avg_salary: avg(select e.salary from partition)
from Employees e
group by  department: e.deptno
having avg(select e.salary from partition) > 30000
```

This gives a set of couples: department and average of the salaries of the employees working in this department, when this average is more than 30000. So the type of the result is

```
bag<struct(department: integer, avg_salary: float)>
```

Note that to compute the average salary, we have used a shortcut notation allowed by the Scope Rules defined in Section 4.9.15. The fully developed notation would read

```
avg_salary: avg(select x.e.salary from partition x)
```

4.9.10 Order-by Operator

If *select_query* is a select-from-where or a select-from-where-group_by query, and if $e_1, e_2, ..., e_n$ are expressions, then *select_query* order by $e_1, e_2, ..., e_n$ is an expression. It returns a list of the selected elements sorted by the functions e_1, and inside each subset yielding the same e_1, sorted by e_2, ..., and the final subsub...set, sorted by e_n.

Example:

```
select p from Persons p order by p.age, p.name
```

This sorts the set of persons on their age, then on their name and puts the sorted objects into the result as a list.

Each sort expression criterion can be followed by the keyword **asc** or **desc**, specifying respectively an ascending or descending order. The default order is that of the previous declaration. For the first expression, the default is ascending.

Example:

```
select * from Persons  order by age desc, name asc, department
```

4.9.11 Indexed Collection Expressions

4.9.11.1 Getting the ith Element of an Indexed Collection

If e_1 and e_2 are expressions, e_1 is a list or an array, e_2 is an integer, then $e_1[e_2]$ is an expression. This extracts the e_2+1 element of the indexed collection e_1. Notice that the first element has the rank 0.

Example:

    list (a,b,c,d) [1]

This returns b.

Example:

    element (select x
            from Courses x
            where x.name = "Math" and x.number ="101").requires[2]

This returns the third prerequisite of Math 101.

4.9.11.2 Extracting a Subcollection of an Indexed Collection

If e_1, e_2, and e_3 are expressions, e_1 is a list or an array, and e_2 and e_3 are integers, then $e_1[e_2:e_3]$ is an expression. This extracts the subcollection of e_1 starting at position e_2 and ending at position e_3.

Example:

    list (a,b,c,d) [1:3]

This returns list (b,c,d).

Example:

    element (select x
            from Courses x
            where x.name="Math" and x.number="101").requires[0:2]

This returns the list consisting of the first three prerequisites of Math 101.

4.9.11.3 Getting the First and Last Elements of an Indexed Collection

If e is an expression, <op> is an operator from {first, last}, and e is a list or an array, then <op>(e) is an expression. This extracts the first and last element of a collection.

Example:

    first(element(select x
                from Courses x
                where x.name="Math" and x.number="101").requires)

This returns the first prerequisite of Math 101.

4.9.11.4 Concatenating Two Indexed Collections

If e_1 and e_2 are expressions and e_1 and e_2 are both lists or both arrays, then e_1+e_2 is an expression. This computes the concatenation of e_1 and e_2.

list (1,2) + list(2,3)

This query generates list (1,2,2,3).

4.9.12 Binary Set Expressions

4.9.12.1 Union, Intersection, Difference

If e_1 and e_2 are expressions, if <op> is an operator from {union, except, intersect}, if e_1 and e_2 are sets or bags, then e_1 <op> e_2 is an expression. This computes set theoretic operations, union, difference, and intersection on e_1 and e_2, as defined in Chapter 2.

When the operand's collection types are different (bag and set), the set is first converted into a bag and the result is a bag.

Examples:

Student except TA

This returns the set of students who are not Teaching Assistants.

bag(2,2,3,3,3) union bag(2,3,3,3)

This bag expression returns bag(2,2,3,3,3,2,3,3,3).

bag(2,2,3,3,3) intersect bag(2,3,3,3)

The intersection of two bags yields a bag that contains the minimum for each of the multiple values. So the result is bag(2,3,3,3).

bag(2,2,3,3,3) except bag(2,3,3,3)

This bag expression returns bag(2).

4.9.12.2 Inclusion

If e_1 and e_2 are expressions which denote sets or bag and if <op> is an operator from {<, <=, >, >=}, then e_1 <op> e_2 is an expression whose value is a boolean.

When the operands are different kinds of collections (bag and set), the set is first converted into a bag.

$e_1 < e_2$ is true if e_1 is included into e_2 but not equal to e_2

$e_1 <= e_2$ is true if e_1 is included into e_2

Example:

set(1,2,3) < set(3,4,2,1) is true

4.9.13   Conversion Expressions

4.9.13.1 Extracting the Element of a Singleton

If e is a collection-valued expression, element(e) is an expression. This takes the singleton e and returns its element. If e is not a singleton this raises an exception.

Example:

element(select x from Professors x where x.name = "Turing")

This returns the professor whose name is Turing (if there is only one).

4.9.13.2 Turning a List into a Set

If e is a list expression, listtoset(e) is an expression. This converts the list into a set, by forming the set containing all the elements of the list.

Example:

listtoset (list(1,2,3,2))

This returns the set containing 1, 2, and 3.

4.9.13.3 Removing Duplicates

If e is an expression whose value is a collection, then distinct(e) is an expression whose value is the same collection after removing the duplicated elements. If e is a bag, distinct(e) is a set. If e is an ordered collection, the relative ordering of the remaining elements is preserved.

4.9.13.4 Flattening Collection of Collections

If e is a collection-valued expression, flatten(e) is an expression. This converts a collection of collections of t into a collection of t. So flattening operates at the first level only.

Assuming the type of e to be $col_1<col_2<t>>$, the result of flatten(e) is:

- If col_2 is a set (resp. a bag), the union of all $col_2<t>$ is done and the result is a set<t> (resp. bag<t>).
- If col_2 is a list or an array and col_1 is a list or an array, the concatenation of all $col_2<t>$ is done following the order in col_1 and the result is $col_2<t>$, which is thus a list or an array. Of course duplicates, if any, are maintained by this operation.
- If col_2 is a list or an array and col_1 is a set (resp. a bag), the lists or arrays are converted into sets (resp. bags), the union of all these sets (resp. bags) is done and the result is a set<t> (resp. bag<t>).

Examples:

flatten(list(set(1,2,3), set(3,4,5,6), set(7)))

This returns the set containing 1,2,3,4,5,6,7.

flatten(list(list(1,2), list(1,2,3)))

This returns list(1,2,1,2,3).

flatten(set(list(1,2), list(1,2,3)))

This returns the set containing 1,2,3.

4.9.13.5 Typing an Expression

If e is an expression and c is a type name, then (c)e is an expression. This asserts that e is an object of class type c.

If it turns out that it is not true, an exception is raised at runtime. This is useful to access a property of an object which is statically known to be of a superclass of the specified class.

Example:

select ((Employee) s).salary
from Students s
where s in (select sec.assistant from Sections sec)

This returns the set of salaries of all students who are teaching assistants, assuming that Students and Sections are the extents of the classes Student and Section.

4.9.14 Function Call

If f is a function name, if e_1 , e_2 , ..., e_n are expressions, then f() and f(e_1, e_2, ..., e_n) are expressions whose value is the value returned by the function, or the object nil, when the function does not return any value. The first form calls a function without a parameter, while the second one calls a function with the parameters e_1, e_2, ..., e_n.

OQL does not define in which language the body of such a function is written. This allows one to extend the functionality of OQL without changing the language.

4.9.15 Scope Rules

The *from* part of a select-from-where query introduces explicit or implicit variables to range over the filtered collections. An example of an explicit variable is

select ... from Persons p ...

while an implicit declaration would be

select ... from Persons ...

The scope of these variables spreads over all the parts of the select-from-where expression including nested sub-expressions.

The *group by* part of a select-from-where-group_by query introduces the name *partition* along with possible explicit attribute names which characterize the partition. These names are visible in the corresponding *having* and *select* parts, including nested sub-expressions within these parts.

Inside a scope, you use these variable names to construct path expressions and reach properties (attributes and operations) when these variables denote complex objects. For instance, in the scope of the first from clause above, you access the age of a person by p.age.

When the variable is implicit, like in the second from clause, you directly use the name of the collection by Persons.age.

However, when no ambiguity exists, you can use the property name directly as a shortcut, without using the variable name to open the scope (this is made implicitly), writing simply: age. There is no ambiguity when a property name is defined for one and only one object denoted by a visible variable.

To summarize, a name appearing in a (nested) query is looked up as follows:

- a variable in the current scope, or
- a named query introduced by the *define* clause, or
- a named object, i.e., an entry point in the database, or
- an attribute name or an operation name of a variable in the current scope, when there is no ambiguity, i.e., this property name belongs to only one variable in the scope.

Example:

Assuming that in the current schema the names Persons and Cities are defined.

```
select  scope1
from    Persons,
        Cities c
where exists(select  scope2 from children as child)
        or count (select scope3, (select scope4 from partition)
              from  children p,
                  scope5 v
              group by  age: scope6
            )
```

In *scope1*, we see the names: Persons, c, Cities, all property names of class Person and class City as long as they are not present in both classes, and they are not called "Persons", "c", nor "Cities".

In *scope2*, we see the names: child, Persons, c, Cities, the property names of the class City which are not property of the class Person. No attribute of the class Person can be accessed directly since they are ambiguous between "child" and "Persons".

In *scope3*, we see the names: age, partition, and the same names from scope1, except "age" and "partition", if they exist.

In *scope4*, we see the names: age, partition, p, v, and the same names from scope1, except "age", "partition", "p" and "v", if they exist.

In *scope5*, we see the names: p, and the same names from scope1, except "p", if it exists.

In *scope6*, we see the names: p, v, Persons, c, Cities, the property names of the class City which are not property of the class Person. No attribute of the class Person can be accessed directly since they are ambiguous between "child" and "Persons".

4.10 Syntactical Abbreviations

OQL defines an orthogonal expression language, in the sense that all operators can be composed with each other as long as the types of the operands are correct. To achieve this property, we have defined a functional language with simple operators such as "+" or composite operators such as "select from where", "group_by", and "order_by" which always deliver a result in the same type system and which thus can be recursively operated with other operations in the same query.

In order to accept the whole DML query part of SQL, as a valid syntax for OQL, we have added ad-hoc constructions each time SQL introduces a syntax which cannot be considered in the category of true operators. This section gives the list of these constructions that we call "abbreviations," since they are completely equivalent to a functional OQL expression. At the same time, we give the semantics of these constructions, since all operators used for this description have been previously defined.

4.10.1 Structure Construction

The structure constructor has been introduced in Section 4.9.4.2. An alternate syntax is allowed in two contexts: select clause and group-by clause. In both contexts, the SQL syntax is accepted, along with the one already defined.

> **select** *projection* {, *projection*} ...
> select ... **group by** *projection* {, *projection*}

where *projection* is one of the forms:

1. expression **as** identifier

2. identifier: expression

3. expression

This is an alternate syntax for

> **struct**(identifier: expression {, identifier: expression})

If there is only one *projection* and the syntax (3) is used in a select clause, then it is not interpreted as a structure construction but rather the expression stands as is. Furthermore, a (3) expression is only valid if it is possible to infer the name of the corresponding attribute (the identifier). This requires that the expression denotes a path expression (possibly of length one) ending by a property whose name is then chosen as the identifier.

Example:

> select p.name, salary, student_id
> from Professors p, p.teaches

This query returns a bag of structures:

> bag<struct(name: string, salary: float, student_id: integer)>

4.10.2 Aggregate Operators

These operators have been introduced in Section 4.9.7.4. SQL adopts a notation which is not functional for them. So OQL accepts this syntax, too. If we define *aggregate* as one of **min**, **max**, **count**, **sum** and **avg**,

> select count(*) from ...   is equivalent to
> count(select * from ...)

> select *aggregate*(query) from ...   is equivalent to
> *aggregate*(select query from ...)

> select *aggregate*(distinct query) from ...   is equivalent to
> *aggregate*(distinct(select query from ...)

4.10.3 Composite Predicates

If e_1 and e_2 are expressions, e_2 is a collection, e_1 has the type of its elements, if *relation* is a relational operator (=, !=, <, <=, > , >=), then e_1 *relation* some e_2 and e_1 *relation* any e_2 and e_1 *relation* all e_2 are expressions whose value is a boolean.

The two first predicates are equivalent to

> exists x in e_2: e_1 *relation* x

The last predicate is equivalent to

>   for all x in e$_2$: e$_1$ *relation* x

Example:

>   10 < some (8,15, 7, 22)   is true

4.10.4   String Literal

OQL accepts single quotes as well to delineate a string (see Section 4.9.3.1), like SQL does. This introduces an ambiguity for a string with one character which then has the same syntax as a character literal. This ambiguity is solved by context.

4.11 OQL BNF

The OQL grammar is given using a rather informal BNF notation.

- •   { symbol } is a sequence of 0 or n symbol(s).
- •   *[*symbol*]* is an optional symbol. Do not confuse this with the separators [].
- •   **keyword** is a terminal of the grammar.
- •   xxx_name is the syntax of an identifier.
- •   xxx_literal is self-explanatory, e.g., "a string" is a string_literal.
- •   bind_argument stands for a parameter when embedded in a programming language, e.g., $3i.

The non-terminal **query** stands for a valid query expression. The grammar is presented as recursive rules producing valid queries. This explains why most of the time this non-terminal appears on the left side of ::=. Of course, each operator expects its "query" operands to be of the right types. These type constraints have been introduced in the previous sections.

These rules must be completed by the priority of OQL operators which is given after the grammar. Some syntactical ambiguities are solved semantically from the types of the operands.

4.11.1 Grammar

4.11.1.1 Axiom (see 4.9.1, 4.9.2)

```
query_program ::=  {define_query;} query
define_query ::=    define identifier as query
```

4.11.1.2 Basic (see 4.9.3)

query ::= **nil**
query ::= **true**
query ::= **false**
query ::= integer_literal
query ::= float_literal
query ::= character_literal
query ::= string_literal
query ::= entry_name
query ::= query_name
query ::= bind_argument[2]
query ::= from_variable_name
query ::= (query)

4.11.1.3 Simple Expression (see 4.9.5)

query ::= query + query[3]
query ::= query - query
query ::= query * query
query ::= query / query
query ::= - query
query ::= query **mod** query
query ::= **abs** (query)
query ::= query II query

4.11.1.4 Comparison (see 4.9.5)

query ::= query comparison_operator query
query ::= query **like** string_literal
comparison_operator ::= =
comparison_operator ::= !=
comparison_operator ::= >
comparison_operator ::= <
comparison_operator ::= >=
comparison_operator ::= <=

4.11.1.5 Boolean Expression (see 4.9.5)

query ::= **not** query
query ::= query **and** query
query ::= query **or** query

---

2. A bind argument allows one to bind expressions from a programming language to a query when embedded into this language (see chapters on language bindings).

3. The operator + is also used for list and array concatenation.

4.11.1.6 Constructor (see 4.9.4)

query ::= type_name (*[*query*]*)
query ::= **type_name** (identifier: query {,identifier: query})
query ::= **struct** (identifier: query {, identifier: query})
query ::= **set** (*[*query {, query}*]*)
query ::= **bag** (*[*query {,query}*]*)
query ::= **list** (*[*query {,query}*]*)
query ::= (query, query {, query})
query ::= *[***list***]*(query .. query)
query ::= **array** (*[*query {,query}*]*)

4.11.1.7 Accessor (see 4.9.6, 4.9.11, 4.9.14, 4.9.15)

query ::= query dot attribute_name
query ::= query dot relationship_name
query ::= query dot operation_name(query {,query})
dot   ::= . | ->
query ::= * query
query ::= query [query]
query ::= query [query:query]
query ::= **first** (query)
query ::= **last** (query)
query ::= function_name(*[*query {,query}*]*)

4.11.1.8 Collection Expression (see 4.9.7, 4.10.3)

query ::= for **all** identifier **in** query: query
query ::= **exists** identifier **in** query: query
query ::= **exists**(query)
query ::= **unique**(query)
query ::= query **in** query
query ::= query comparison_operator quantifier query
quantifier ::= **some**
quantifier ::= **any**
quantifier ::= **all**
query ::= **count** (query)
query ::= **count** (*)
query ::= **sum** (query)
query ::= **min** (query)
query ::= **max** (query)
query ::= **avg** (query)

4.11.1.9 Select Expression (see 4.9.8, 4.9.9, 4.9.10)

> query ::= **select** [**distinct**] projection_attributes
>   **from** variable_declaration {, variable_declaration}
>   [**where** query]
>   [**group by** partition_attributes]
>   [**having** query]
>   [**order by** sort_criterion {, sort_criterion}]
> projection_attributes ::= projection {, projection}
> projection_attributes ::= *
> projection ::= query
> projection ::= identifier: query
> projection ::= query **as** identifier
> variable_declaration ::= query [[**as**] identifier]
> partition_attributes ::= projection {, projection}
> sort_criterion ::= query [ordering]
> ordering ::= **asc**
> ordering ::= **desc**

4.11.1.10 Set Expression (see 4.9.12)

> query ::= query **intersect** query
> query ::= query **union** query
> query ::= query **except** query

4.11.1.11 Conversion (see 4.9.13)

> query ::= **listtoset** (query)
> query ::= **element** (query)
> query ::= **distinct**(e)
> query ::= **flatten** (query)
> query ::= (class_name) query

4.11.2 Operator Priorities

The following operators are sorted by decreasing priority. Operators on the same line have the same priority and group left-to-right.

() [] . ->
not - (unary) + (unary)
in
* / mod intersect
+ - union except ||
< > <= >= < some < any < all   (etc. ... for all comparison operators)
= != like
and exists for all
or
.. :
,
(identifier) this is the cast operator
order
having
group by
where
from
select

Chapter 5

C++ Binding

5.1 Introduction

This chapter defines the C++ binding for ODL/OML.

ODL stands for Object Definition Language. It is the declarative portion of C++ ODL/OML. The C++ binding of ODL is expressed as a library which provides classes and functions to implement the concepts defined in the ODMG object model. OML stands for Object Manipulation Language. It is the language used for retrieving objects from the database and modifying them. The C++ OML syntax and semantics are those of standard C++ in the context of the standard class library.

ODL/OML specifies only the logical characteristics of objects and the operations used to manipulate them. It does not discuss the physical storage of objects. It does not address the clustering or memory management issues associated with the stored physical representation of objects or access structures like indices used to accelerate object retrieval. In an ideal world these would be transparent to the programmer. In the real world they are not. An additional set of constructs called *physical pragmas* is defined to give the programmer some direct control over these issues, or at least to enable a programmer to provide "hints" to the storage management subsystem provided as part of the ODBMS runtime. Physical pragmas exist within the ODL and OML. They are added to object type definitions specified in ODL, expressed as OML operations, or shown as optional arguments to operations defined within OML. Because these pragmas are not in any sense a stand-alone language, but rather a set of constructs added to ODL/OML to address implementation issues, they are included within the relevant subsections of this chapter.

The chapter is organized as follows. Section 5.2 discusses the ODL. Section 5.3 discusses the OML. Section 5.4 discusses OQL — the distinguished subset of OML that supports associative retrieval. Associative retrieval is access based on the values of the properties of objects rather than on their IDs or names. Section 5.5 provides an example program.

5.1.1 Language Design Principles

The programming language–specific bindings for ODL/OML defined in Chapters 5 and 6 of this document, for C++ and Smalltalk respectively, are based on one basic principle: The programmer feels that there is one language, not two separate languages with arbitrary boundaries between them. This principle has two corollaries that are evident in the design of the C++ binding defined in the body of this chapter:

1. There is a single unified type system across the programming language and the database; individual instances of these common types can be persistent or transient.

2. The programming language–specific binding for ODL/OML respects the syntax and semantics of the base programming language into which it is being inserted.

5.1.2 Language Binding

The C++ binding maps the Object Model into C++ by introducing a set of classes that can have both persistent and transient instances. These classes are informally referred to as "persistence-capable classes" in the body of this chapter. These classes are distinct from the normal classes defined by the C++ language, all of whose instances are transient; that is, they don't outlive the execution of the process in which they were created. Where it is necessary to distinguish between these two categories of classes, the former are called "persistence-capable classes"; the latter are referred to as "transient classes."

The C++ to ODBMS language binding approach described by this standard is based on the smart pointer or "Ref-based" approach. For each persistence-capable class T, an ancillary class d_Ref<T> is defined. Instances of persistence-capable classes are then referenced using parameterized references, e.g.,

```
(1)  d_Ref<Professor>    profP;
(2)  d_Ref<Department>   deptRef;
(3)  profP->grant_tenure();
(4)  deptRef = profP->dept;
```

Statement (1) declares the object profP as an instance of the type d_Ref<Professor>. Statement (2) declares deptRef as an instance of the type d_Ref<Department>. Statement (3) invokes the grant_tenure operation defined on class Professor, on the instance of that class referred to by profP. Statement (4) assigns the value of the dept attribute of the professor referenced by profP to the variable deptRef.

Instances of persistence-capable classes may contain embedded members of C++ built-in types, user-defined classes, or pointers to transient data. Applications may refer to such embedded members using C++ pointers (*) or references (&) only during the execution of a transaction.

In this chapter we use the following terms to describe the places where the standard is formally considered undefined or allows for an implementor of one of the bindings to make implementation-specific decisions with respect to implementing the standard. The terms are

> *Undefined:* The behavior is unspecified by the standard. Implementations have complete freedom (can do anything or nothing), and the behavior need not be documented by the implementor or vendor.

> *Implementation-defined:* The behavior is specified by each implementor/vendor. The implementor/vendor is allowed to make implementation-specific decisions about the behavior. However, the behavior must be well defined and fully documented and published as part of the vendor's implementation of the standard.

Figure 5-1 shows the hierarchy of languages involved, as well as the preprocess, compile, and link steps that generate an executable application.

5.1.3 Mapping the ODMG Object Model into C++

Although C++ provides a powerful data model that is close to the one presented in Chapter 2, it is worth trying to explain more precisely how concepts introduced in Chapter 2 map into concrete C++ constructs.

5.1.3.1 Object and Literal

An ODMG object type maps into a C++ class. Depending on how a C++ class is instantiated, the result can be an ODMG object or an ODMG literal. A C++ object embedded as a member within an enclosing class is treated as an ODMG literal. This is explained by the fact that a block of memory is inserted into the enclosing object and belongs entirely to it. For instance, one cannot copy the enclosing object without getting a copy of the embedded one at the same time. In this sense the embedded object cannot be considered as having an identity, since it acts as a literal.

5.1.3.2 Structure

The Object Model notion of a *structure* maps into the C++ construct *struct* or *class* embedded in a class.

5.1.3.3 Implementation

C++ has implicit the notion of dividing a class definition into two parts: its interface (public part) and its implementation (protected and private members and function definitions). However, in C++ only one implementation is possible for a given class.

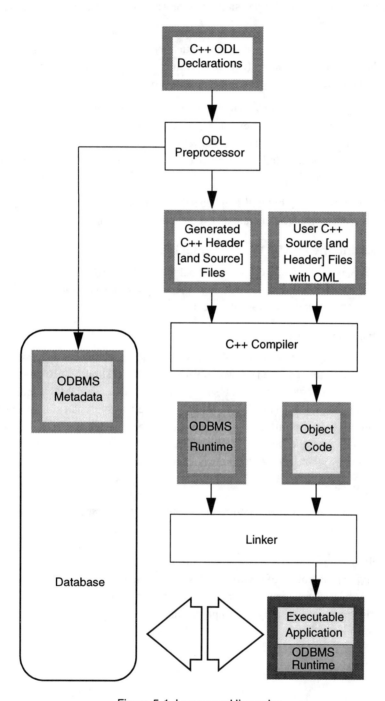

Figure 5-1. Language Hierarchy

5.1.3.4 Collection Classes

The ODMG object model includes collection type generators, collection types, and collection instances. Collection type generators are represented as *template classes* in C++. Collection types are represented as collection classes, and collection instances are represented as instances of these collection classes. To illustrate these three categories:

```
template<class T> class d_Set : public d_Collection<T> { ... };
class Ship { ... };
d_Set<d_Ref<Ship> >  Cunard_Line;
```

d_Set<T> is a collection template class. d_Set<d_Ref<Ship> > is a collection class. And Cunard_Line is a particular collection, an instance of the class d_Set<d_Ref<Ship> >.

The subtype/supertype hierarchy of collection types defined in the ODMG Object Model (Section 2.6.3) is directly carried over into C++. The type d_Collection<T> is an abstract class in C++ with no direct instances. It is instantiable only through its derived classes. The only differences between the collection classes in the C++ binding and their counterparts in Section 2.6.3 are the following:

- Named operations in the Object Model are mapped to C++ function members.
- For some operations, the C++ binding includes both the named function and an overloaded infix operation, e.g., d_Set::union_with also has the form operator+=. The statements s1.union_with(s2) and s1 += s2 are functionally equivalent.
- Operations that return a boolean in Section 2.6.3 are modeled as function members that return an int in the C++ binding. This is done to match the C convention that a zero-valued int means false; any other value is true.
- The create and delete operations defined in Section 2.6.3 have been replaced with C++ constructors and destructors.

5.1.3.5 Array

C++ provides a syntax for creating and accessing a contiguous and indexable sequence of objects. This has been chosen to map partially to the ODMG Array collection. To complement it, a d_Varray C++ class is also provided, which implements an array whose upper bound may vary with time.

5.1.3.6 Relationship

Relationships are not directly supported by C++. Instead, they are supported in ODMG by including instances of specific template classes which provide the maintenance of the relationship.

The relation itself is implemented as a reference (one-to-one relation) or as a collection (one-to-many relation) embedded in the object.

5.1.3.7 Extents

Extents are not directly supported by C++. The programmer is responsible for defining a collection and writing methods that maintain it.

5.1.3.8 Keys

Key declarations are not supported by C++.

5.1.3.9 Names

In the C++ binding an object can acquire only one name, while in the ODMG model more than one name may refer to the same object. An attempt to associate more than one name with an object will cause a d_Error exception object of kind d_Error_NameNotUnique to be thrown.

5.1.3.10 Database Administration

Some operations regarding database administration are intentionally omitted from the C++ binding. For instance the C++ binding does not provide a means to create a database nor to define an index on a collection.

5.1.4 Use of C++ Language Features

5.1.4.1 Prefix

The global names in the ODMG interface will have a prefix of d_. The intention is to avoid name collisions with other names in the global namespace. The ODMG will keep the prefix even after C++ namespaces are generally available.

5.1.4.2 Namespaces

The namespace feature added to C++ did not have generally available implementations at the time this specification was written. In the future the ODMG plans to utilize namespaces and intends to use odmg as their namespace name.

5.1.4.3 Exception Handling

When error conditions are detected, an instance of class d_Error is thrown using the standard C++ exception mechanism. Class d_Error is derived from the class exception defined in the C++ standard.

Instances of d_Error contain state describing the cause of the error. This state is composed of a number, representing the kind of error, and optional additional information. This additional information can be appended to the error object by using operator<<. If the d_Error object is caught, more information can be appended to it, if it is to be thrown again. The complete state of the object is returned as a human-readable character string by the what function.

The d_Error class is defined as follows.

```
class d_Error : public exception {
public:
    typedef d_Long    kind;
                      d_Error();
                      d_Error(const d_Error &);
                      d_Error(kind the_kind);
                      ~d_Error();
    kind              get_kind();
    void              set_kind(kind the_kind);
    const char *      what() const throw();

    d_Error &         operator<<(d_Char);
    d_Error &         operator<<(d_Short);
    d_Error &         operator<<(d_UShort);
    d_Error &         operator<<(d_Long);
    d_Error &         operator<<(d_ULong);
    d_Error &         operator<<(d_Float);
    d_Error &         operator<<(d_Double);
    d_Error &         operator<<(const char *);
    d_Error &         operator<<(const d_String &);
    d_Error &         operator<<(const d_Error &);
};
```

The following constants are defined for error kinds used in this standard.

- d_Error_DatabaseClassMismatch
- d_Error_DatabaseClassUndefined
- d_Error_DatabaseClosed
- d_Error_DatabaseOpen
- d_Error_DateInvalid
- d_Error_IteratorExhausted
- d_Error_NameNotUnique
- d_Error_QueryParameterCountInvalid
- d_Error_QueryParameterTypeInvalid
- d_Error_RefInvalid
- d_Error_RefNull
- d_Error_TimeInvalid

- d_Error_TimestampInvalid
- d_Error_TransactionOpen
- d_Error_TypeInvalid

5.1.4.4 Preprocessor Identifier

A preprocessor identifier, _ _ODMG_93_ _ , is defined for conditional compilation.

5.1.4.5 Implementation Extensions

Implementations must provide the full function signatures for all the interface methods specified in the chapter and may provide variants on these methods, with additional parameters. Each additional parameter must have a default value. This allows applications that do not use the additional parameters to be portable.

5.2 C++ ODL

This section defines the C++ Object Definition Language. C++ ODL provides a description of the database schema as a set of object classes — including their attributes, relationships, and operations — in a syntactic style that is consistent with that of the declarative portion of a C++ program. Instances of these classes can be manipulated through the C++ OML.

Following is an example declaring type Professor.

```
extern const char _professors[ ];
extern const char _advisor [ ];

class Professor : public d_Object {
public:
// properties:
    d_UShort                            age;
    d_UShort                            id_number;
    d_String                            office_number;
    d_String                            name;
    d_Rel_Ref<Department, _professors>  dept;
    d_Rel_Set<Student, _advisor>        advisees;
// operations:
    void                                grant_tenure();
    void                                assign_course(Course &);
private:

            ...
};

const char _professors [ ] = "professors";
const char _advisor [ ] = "advisor";
```

The syntax for a C++ ODL class declaration is identical to a C++ class declaration. Attribute declarations map to a restricted set of C++ data member declarations. The variables _professors and _advisor are used for establishing an association between the two ends of a relationship.

Static data members of classes are not contained within each individual instance but are of static storage class. Thus static data members are not stored in the database, but are supported for persistence-capable classes. Supertypes are specified using the standard C++ syntax within the class header, e.g., class Professor : public Employee. Though this specification may use public members for ease and brevity, private and protected members are supported.

5.2.1 Attribute Declarations

Attribute declarations are syntactically identical to data member declarations within C++. Because notions of attributes as objects are not yet defined and included in this standard, attributes and data members are not and cannot be syntactically distinguished. In this standard, an attribute cannot have properties (e.g., unit of measure) and there is no way to specialize the get_value and set_value operations defined on the type (e.g., to raise an event when a value is changed).

Standard C++ syntax and semantics for class definitions are supported. However, compliant implementations need not support the following data types within persistent classes:

- unions
- bit fields
- references(&)

as members. Unions and bit fields pose problems when supporting heterogeneous environments. The semantics of references is that they are initialized once at creation; all subsequent operations are directed to the referenced object. References within persistent objects cannot be re-initialized when brought from the database into memory and their initialization value would, in general, not be valid across process boundaries. A set of special classes is defined within the ODMG specification to contain references to persistent objects.

In addition to all primitive data types, except those noted above, structures and class objects can be members. There are several structured literal types that are provided. These include

- d_String
- d_Interval
- d_Date
- d_Time
- d_Timestamp

Examples:

```
struct University_Address {
        d_UShort     PO_box;
        d_String     university;
        d_String     city;
        d_String     state;
        d_String     zip_code;
};


class Student : public d_Object {
public:
        d_String               name;
        d_Date                 birth_date;
        Phone_Number           dorm_phone;
        University_Address     address;
        d_List<d_String>       favorite_friends;
};
```

The attribute name takes a d_String as its value. The attribute dorm_phone takes a user-defined type Phone_Number as its value. The attribute address takes a structure. The attribute favorite_friends takes a d_List of Strings as its value. The following sections contain descriptions of the provided literal types.

5.2.1.1 Fixed-Length Types

In addition to the C++ built-in data types, such as the signed, unsigned, and floating point numeric data types, the following fixed length types will be supported for use in defining attributes of persistence capable classes.

Type Name	Range	Description
d_Short	16 bit	signed integer
d_Long	32 bit	signed integer
d_UShort	16 bit	unsigned integer
d_ULong	32 bit	unsigned integer
d_Float	32 bit	IEEE Std 754-1985 single-precision floating point
d_Double	64 bit	IEEE Std 754-1985 double-precision floating point
d_Char	8 bit	ASCII
d_Octet	8 bit	no interpretation
d_Boolean	0 or 1	defines false(0) and true(1)

Unlike the C++ built-in types, these types have the same range and interpretation on all platforms and environments. Use of these types is recommended when developing applications targeted for heterogeneous environments. Note that like all other global names described in this chapter, these types will be defined within the ODMG namespace when that feature becomes available.

Any ODMG implementation which allows access to a database from applications that have been constructed with different assumptions about the range or interpretation of the C++ built-in types may require the use of the fixed-length data types listed above when defining attributes of persistent objects. The behavior of the database system in such a heterogeneous environment when the C++ built-in types are used for persistent data attributes is undefined.

ODMG implementations will allow but not require the use of the fixed-length data types when used in homogeneous environments.

For any given C++ language environment or platform, these fixed-length data types may be defined as identical to a built-in C++ data type that conforms to the range and interpretation requirements. Since a given C++ built-in data type may meet the requirements in some environments but not in others, portable application code should not assume any correspondence nor lack of correspondence between the fixed-length data types and similar C++ built-in data types. In particular, function overloads should not be disambiguated solely on the difference between a fixed-length data type and a closely corresponding C++ built-in data type. Also, different implementations of a virtual function should use signatures that correspond exactly to the declaration in the base class with respect to use of fixed-length data types vs. C++ built-in data types.

5.2.1.2 d_String

The following class defines a literal type to be used for string attributes. It is intended that this class is used strictly for storing strings in the database, as opposed to being a general string class with all the functionality of a string class normally used for transient strings in an application.

Initialization, assignment, copying, and conversion to and from C++ character strings are supported. The comparison operators are defined on d_String to compare either with another d_String or a C++ character string. One can also access an element in the d_String via an index and also determine the length of the d_String.

Definition:

```
class d_String {
public:
                    d_String();
                    d_String(const d_String &);
                    d_String(const char *);
```

```
                              ~d_String();
        d_String &            operator=(const d_String &);
        d_String &            operator=(const char *);
                              operator const char *() const;
        char &                operator[](unsigned long index);
        unsigned long         length() const;
  friend int                  operator==(const d_String &sL, const d_String &sR);
  friend int                  operator==(const d_String &sL, const char *pR);
  friend int                  operator==(const char *pL, const d_String &sR);
  friend int                  operator!=(const d_String &sL, const d_String &sR);
  friend int                  operator!=(const d_String &sL, const char *pR);
  friend int                  operator!=(const char *pL, const d_String &sR);
  friend int                  operator<  (const d_String &sL, const d_String &sR);
  friend int                  operator<  (const d_String &sL, const char *pR);
  friend int                  operator<  (const char *pL, const d_String &sR);
  friend int                  operator<=(const d_String &sL, const d_String &sR);
  friend int                  operator<=(const d_String &sL, const char *pR);
  friend int                  operator<=(const char *pL, const d_String &sR);
  friend int                  operator>  (const d_String &sL, const d_String &sR);
  friend int                  operator>  (const d_String &sL, const char *pR);
  friend int                  operator>  (const char *pL, const d_String &sR);
  friend int                  operator>=(const d_String &sL, const d_String &sR);
  friend int                  operator>=(const d_String &sL, const char *pR);
  friend int                  operator>=(const char *pL, const d_String &sR);
  };
```

5.2.1.3 d_Interval

The d_Interval class is used to represent a duration of time. It is also used to perform arithmetic operations on the d_Date, d_Time, and d_Timestamp classes. This class corresponds to the day-time interval as defined in the SQL standard.

Initialization, assignment, arithmetic, and comparison functions are defined on the class, as well as member functions to access the time components of its current value.

The d_Interval class accepts non-normalized input, but normalizes the time components when accessed. For example, the constructor would accept 28 hours as input, but then calling the day function would return a value of 1 and the hour function would return a value of 4. Arithmetic would work in a similar manner.

Definition:

```
class d_Interval {
public:
                        d_Interval(int day = 0, int hour = 0,int min = 0, float sec = 0.0);
                        d_Interval(const d_Interval &);
        d_Interval &    operator=(const d_Interval &);
        int             day() const;
        int             hour() const;
        int             minute() const;
        float           second() const;
        int             is_zero() const;
        d_Interval &    operator+=(const d_Interval &);
        d_Interval &    operator-=(const d_Interval &);
        d_Interval &    operator*=(int);
        d_Interval &    operator/=(int);
        d_Interval      operator-() const;
    friend  d_Interval  operator+(const d_Interval &L, const d_Interval &R);
    friend  d_Interval  operator-(const d_Interval &L, const d_Interval &R);
    friend  d_Interval  operator*(const d_Interval &L, int R);
    friend  d_Interval  operator*(int L, const d_Interval &R);
    friend  d_Interval  operator/ (const d_Interval &L, int R);
    friend  int         operator==(const d_Interval &L, const d_Interval &R);
    friend  int         operator!= (const d_Interval &L, const d_Interval &R);
    friend  int         operator<  (const d_Interval &L, const d_Interval &R);
    friend  int         operator<=(const d_Interval &L, const d_Interval &R);
    friend  int         operator>  (const d_Interval &L, const d_Interval &R);
    friend  int         operator>=(const d_Interval &L, const d_Interval &R);
};
```

5.2.1.4 d_Date

The d_Date class stores a representation of a date consisting of a year, month, and day. It also provides enumerations to denote weekdays and months.

Initialization, assignment, arithmetic, and comparison functions are provided. Implementations may have additional functions available to support converting to and from the type used by the operating system to represent a date. Functions are provided to access the components of a date. There are also functions to determine the number of days in a month, etc. The static function current returns the current date. The next and previous functions advance the date to the next specified weekday.

Definition:

```
class d_Date {
public:
    enum Weekday {
        Sunday = 0,      Monday = 1,     Tuesday = 2,     Wednesday = 3,
        Thursday = 4,    Friday = 5,     Saturday = 6
    };
    enum Month {
        January = 1,  February = 2,  March = 3,  April = 4,  May = 5,   June = 6,
        July = 7,   August = 8,   September = 9,   October = 10,   November = 11,
        December = 12
    };
                        d_Date();          // sets to current date
                        d_Date(unsigned short year, unsigned short day_of_year);
                        d_Date(unsigned short year, unsigned short month,
                                unsigned short day);
                        d_Date(const d_Date &);
                        d_Date(const d_Timestamp &);
    d_Date &            operator=(const d_Date &);
    d_Date &            operator=(const d_Timestamp &);
    unsigned short      year() const;
    unsigned short      month() const;
    unsigned short      day() const;
    unsigned short      day_of_year() const;
    Weekday             day_of_week() const;
    Month               month_of_year() const;
    int                 is_leap_year() const;
    static int          is_leap_year(unsigned short year);
    static d_Date       current();
    d_Date &            next(Weekday);
    d_Date &            previous(Weekday);
    d_Date &            operator+=(const d_Interval &);
    d_Date &            operator+=(int ndays);
    d_Date &            operator++();      // prefix  ++d
    d_Date              operator++(int);   // postfix d++
    d_Date &            operator-=(const d_Interval &);
    d_Date &            operator-=(int ndays);
    d_Date &            operator--();      // prefix  --d
    d_Date              operator--(int);   // postfix d--
    friend d_Date       operator+(const d_Date &L, const d_Interval &R);
```

friend d_Date	operator+(const d_Interval &L, const d_Date &R);
friend d_Date	operator–(const d_Date &L, const d_Interval &R);
friend int	operator==(const d_Date &L, const d_Date &R);
friend int	operator!= (const d_Date &L, const d_Date &R);
friend int	operator< (const d_Date &L, const d_Date &R);
friend int	operator<=(const d_Date &L, const d_Date &R);
friend int	operator> (const d_Date &L, const d_Date &R);
friend int	operator>=(const d_Date &L, const d_Date &R);
int	is_between(const d_Date &, const d_Date &) const;
friend int	overlaps(const d_Date &psL, const d_Date &peL, const d_Date &psR, const d_Date &peR);
friend int	overlaps(const d_Timestamp &sL, const d_Timestamp &eL, const d_Date &sR, const d_Date &eR);
friend int	overlaps(const d_Date &sL, const d_Date &eL, const d_Timestamp &sR, const d_Timestamp &eR);
static int	days_in_year(unsigned short year);
int	days_in_year() const;
static int	days_in_month(unsigned short yr, unsigned short month);
int	days_in_month() const;
static int	is_valid_date(unsigned short year, unsigned short month, unsigned short day);

```
};
```

If an attempt is made to set a d_Date object to an invalid value, a d_Error exception object of kind d_Error_DateInvalid is thrown and the value of the d_Date object is undefined.

The functions next, previous, operator+= and operator–= alter the object and return a reference to the current object. Exceptions are the post increment and decrement operators, which return a new object by value.

The overlaps functions take two periods(start and end), each period denoted by a start and end time, and determines whether the two time periods overlap. The is_between function determines whether the d_Date value is within a given period.

5.2.1.5 d_Time

The d_Time class is used to denote a specific time, which is internally stored in Greenwich Mean Time (GMT). Initialization, assignment, arithmetic, and comparison operators are defined. There are also functions to access each of the components of a time value. Implementations may have additional functions available to support converting to and from the type used by the operating system to represent a time.

The enumeration Time_Zone is made available to denote a specific time zone. Time zones are numbered according to the number of hours which must be added or subtracted from local time to get the time in Greenwich, England (GMT). Thus the value of GMT is 0. A Time_Zone name of GMT6 indicates a time of 6 hours greater than GMT and thus 6 must be subtracted from it to get GMT. Conversely, GMT_8 means that the time is 8 hours earlier than GMT (read the underscore as a minus). A default time zone value is maintained and is initially set to the local time zone. It is possible to change the default time zone value as well as reset it to the local value.

Definition:

```
class d_Time {
public:
    enum Time_Zone {
        GMT  = 0,   GMT12 = 12,    GMT_12 = -12,
        GMT1 = 1,   GMT_1 = -1,    GMT2 = 2,     GMT_2 = -2,
        GMT3 = 3,   GMT_3 = -3,    GMT4 = 4,     GMT_4 = -4,
        GMT5 = 5,   GMT_5 = -5,    GMT6 = 6,     GMT_6 = -6,
        GMT7 = 7,   GMT_7 = -7,    GMT8 = 8,     GMT_8 = -8,
        GMT9 = 9,   GMT_9 = -9,    GMT10 = 10,   GMT_10 = -10,
        GMT11 = 11, GMT_11 = -11,
        USeastern = -5,   UScentral = -6,  USmountain = -7,  USpacific = -8
    };
    static   void            set_default_Time_Zone(Time_Zone);
    static   void            set_default_Time_Zone_to_local();
                             d_Time();
                             d_Time(unsigned short hour,
                                    unsigned short minute, float sec);
                             d_Time(unsigned short hour, unsigned short minute,
                                    float sec, short tzhour, short tzminute);
                             d_Time(const d_Time &);
                             d_Time(const d_Timestamp &);
    d_Time &                 operator=(const d_Time &);
    d_Time &                 operator=(const d_Timestamp &);
    unsigned short           hour() const;
    unsigned short           minute() const;
    float                    second() const;
    short                    tz_hour() const;
    short                    tz_minute() const;
    static  d_Time           current();
    d_Time &                 operator+=(const d_Interval &);
    d_Time &                 operator-=(const d_Interval &);
```

friend d_Time	operator+(const d_Time &L, const d_Interval &R);
friend d_Time	operator+(const d_Interval &L, const d_Time &R);
friend d_Interval	operator−(const d_Time &L, const d_Time &R);
friend d_Time	operator−(const d_Time &L, const d_Interval &R);
friend int	operator==(const d_Time &L, const d_Time &R);
friend int	operator!= (const d_Time &L, const d_Time &R);
friend int	operator< (const d_Time &L, const d_Time &R);
friend int	operator<=(const d_Time &L, const d_Time &R);
friend int	operator> (const d_Time &L, const d_Time &R);
friend int	operator>=(const d_Time &L, const d_Time &R);
friend int	overlaps(const d_Time &psL, const d_Time &peL,
	const d_Time &psR, const d_Time &peR);
friend int	overlaps(const d_Timestamp &sL, const d_Timestamp &eL,
	const d_Time &sR, const d_Time &eR);
friend int	overlaps(const d_Time &sL, const d_Time &eL,
	const d_Timestamp &sR, const d_Timestamp &eR);

};

All arithmetic on d_Time is done on a modulo 24 hour basis. If an attempt is made to set a d_Time object to an invalid value, a d_Error exception object of kind d_Error_TimeInvalid is thrown and the value of the d_Time object is undefined.

The default d_Time constructor initializes the object to the current time. The overlaps functions take two periods, each denoted by a start and end time, and determines whether the two time periods overlap.

5.2.1.6 d_Timestamp

A d_Timestamp consists of both a date and time.

Definition:

```
class d_Timestamp {
public:
                    d_Timestamp();     // sets to the current date/time
                    d_Timestamp(unsigned short year, unsigned short month= 1,
                        unsigned short day = 1, unsigned short hour = 0,
                        unsigned short minute = 0, float sec = 0.0);
                    d_Timestamp(const d_Date &);
                    d_Timestamp(const d_Date &, const d_Time &);
                    d_Timestamp(const d_Timestamp &);
    d_Timestamp &   operator=(const d_Timestamp &);
    d_Timestamp &   operator=(const d_Date &);
```

```
        d_Date &        date();
        const d_Time &  time() const;
        unsigned short  year() const;
        unsigned short  month() const;
        unsigned short  day() const;
        unsigned short  hour() const;
        unsigned short  minute() const;
        float           second() const;
        short           tz_hour() const;
        short           tz_minute() const;

    static  d_Timestamp  current();
        d_Timestamp &   operator+=(const d_Interval &);
        d_Timestamp &   operator-=(const d_Interval &);
    friend  d_Timestamp  operator+(const d_Timestamp &L, const d_Interval &R);
    friend  d_Timestamp  operator+(const d_Interval &L, const d_Timestamp &R);
    friend  d_Timestamp  operator-(const d_Timestamp &L, const d_Interval &R);
    friend  int         operator==(const d_Timestamp &L, const d_Timestamp &R);
    friend  int         operator!=(const d_Timestamp &L, const d_Timestamp &R);
    friend  int         operator< (const d_Timestamp &L, const d_Timestamp &R);
    friend  int         operator<=(const d_Timestamp &L, const d_Timestamp &R);
    friend  int         operator> (const d_Timestamp &L, const d_Timestamp &R);
    friend  int         operator>=(const d_Timestamp &L, const d_Timestamp &R);
    friend  int         overlaps(const d_Timestamp &sL, const d_Timestamp &eL,
                                const d_Timestamp &sR, const d_Timestamp &eR);
    friend  int         overlaps(const d_Timestamp &sL, const d_Timestamp &eL,
                                const d_Date &sR, const d_Date &eR);
    friend  int         overlaps(const d_Date &sL, const d_Date &eL,
                                const d_Timestamp &sR, const d_Timestamp &eR);
    friend  int         overlaps(const d_Timestamp &sL, const d_Timestamp &eL,
                                const d_Time &sR, const d_Time &eR);
    friend  int         overlaps(const d_Time &sL, const d_Time &eL,
                                const d_Timestamp &sR, const d_Timestamp &eR);
};
```

If an attempt is made to set the value of a d_Timestamp object to an invalid value, a
d_Error exception object of kind d_Error_TimestampInvalid is thrown and the value of
the d_Timestamp object is undefined.

5.2.2 Relationship Traversal Path Declarations

Relationships do not have syntactically separate definitions. Instead, the *traversal
paths* used to cross relationships are defined within the bodies of the definitions of each

of the two object types that serve a role in the relationship. For example, if there is a one-to-many relationship between professors and the students they have as advisees, then the traversal path advisees is defined within the type definition of the object type Professor, and the traversal path advisor is defined within the type definition of the object type Student.

A relationship traversal path declaration is similar to an attribute declaration, but with the following differences. Each end of a relationship has a relationship traversal path. A traversal path declaration is an attribute declaration and must be of type

- d_Rel_Ref<T, const char *> (which has the interface of d_Ref<T>)
- d_Rel_Set<T, const char *> (which has the interface of d_Set<d_Ref<T> >)
- d_Rel_List<T, const char *> (which has the interface of d_List<d_Ref<T> >)

for some persistent class T. The second template argument should be a variable which contains the name of the attribute in the other class which serves as the inverse role in the relationship. Both classes in a relationship must have a member of one of these types and the members of the two classes must refer to each other. Studying the relationships in the examples below will make this clear.

Examples:

```
extern const char _dept [ ],      _professors [ ] ;
extern const char _advisor [ ],   _advisees [ ] ;
extern const char _classes [ ],   _enrolled [ ] ;

class Department : public d_Object {
public:
     d_Rel_Set<Professor, _dept>          professors;
};
class Professor : public d_Object {
public:
     d_Rel_Ref<Department, _professors>   dept;
     d_Rel_Set<Student, _advisor>         advisees;
};
class Student : public d_Object {
public:
     d_Rel_Ref<Professor, _advisees>      advisor;
     d_Rel_Set<Course, _enrolled>         classes;
};
class Course : public d_Object {
public:
     d_Rel_Set<Student, _classes>         students_enrolled;
};
```

```
const char _dept [ ] = "dept";
const char _professors [ ] = "professors";
const char _advisor [ ] = "advisor";
const char _advisees [ ] = "advisees";
const char _classes [ ] = "classes" ;
const char _enrolled [ ] = "students_enrolled";
```

The second template parameter is based on the address of the variable, not on the string contents. Thus a different variable is required for each role, even if the member name happens to be the same. The string contents must match the name of the member in the other class involved in the relationship.

The referential integrity of bidirectional relationships is automatically maintained. If a relationship exists between two objects and one of the objects gets deleted, the relationship is considered to no longer exist and the inverse traversal path will be altered to remove the relationship.

5.2.3 Unidirectional Relationship Declarations

In order to accommodate a common practice in C++ programming, a degenerate form of a relationship is allowed, that which specifies a one-way path. The syntax for the declaration of unidirectional relationships is indistinguishable from the C++ syntax for declaring members of type d_Ref or any concrete subclass of d_Collection that contains references (d_Ref) to persistent objects.

The application is responsible for maintaining the relationship consistently when the object(s) at the end of the path is (are) deleted. No referential integrity maintenance is performed for unidirectional relationships.

Such unidirectional relationship declarations are allowed both inside a class and inside embedded structured attributes.

Examples:

```
struct Responsible {
    d_String                dept;
    d_Ref<Employee>         e;
    d_Date                  due_date;
};


class Order {
public:
    d_Set<d_Ref<Client> >   who;
    d_String                what;
    Responsible             contact;
};
```

5.2.4 Operation Declarations

Operation declarations in C++ are syntactically identical to *function member* declarations. For example, see grant_tenure and assign_course defined for class Professor in Section 5.2.

5.3 C++ OML

This section describes the C++ binding for the OML. A guiding principle in the design of C++ OML is that the syntax used to create, delete, identify, reference, get/set property values, and invoke operations on a persistent object should be, so far as possible, no different than that used for objects of shorter lifetimes. A single expression may freely intermix references to persistent and transient objects.

While it is our long-term goal that nothing can be done with persistent objects that cannot also be done with transient objects, this standard treats persistent and transient objects slightly differently. Queries and transaction consistency apply only to persistent objects.

5.3.1 Object Creation, Deletion, Modification, and References

Objects can be created, deleted, and modified. Objects are created in C++ OML using the new operator, which is overloaded to accept additional arguments specifying the lifetime of the object. An optional storage pragma allows the programmer to specify how the newly allocated object is to be clustered with respect to other objects.

The static member variable d_Database::transient_memory is defined in order to allow libraries that create objects to be used uniformly to create objects of any lifetime. This variable may be used as the value of the database argument to operator new to create objects of transient lifetime.

```
static const d_Database * const d_Database::transient_memory;
```

The formal ODMG forms of the C++ new operator are

```
(1) void * operator new(size_t size);
(2) void * operator new(size_t size, const d_Ref_Any &clustering,
                        const char* typename);
(3) void * operator new(size_t size, d_Database *database,
                        const char* typename);
```

These operators have d_Object scope for those implementations that actually introduce a d_Object class. (1) is used for creation of transient objects derived from d_Object. (2) and (3) create persistent objects. In (2) the user specifies that the newly created object should be placed "near" the existing clustering object. The exact interpretation of "near" is implementation-defined. An example interpretation would be "on the same page if possible." In (3) the user specifies that the newly created object should be placed in the specified database, but no further clustering is specified.

The size argument, which appears as the first argument in each signature, is the size of the representation of an object. It is determined by the compiler as a function of the class of which the new object is an instance, not passed as an explicit argument by a programmer writing in the language.

If the database does not have the schema information about a class when new is called a d_Error exception object of kind d_Error_DatabaseClassUndefined is thrown.

Examples:

```
        d_Database *yourDB, *myDB;  // assume these get initialized properly
(1)    d_Ref<Schedule> temp_sched1 = new Schedule;
(2)    d_Ref<Professor> prof2 = new(yourDB,"Professor") Professor;
(3)    d_Ref<Student> student1 = new(myDB, "Student") Student;
(4)    d_Ref<Student> student2 = new(student1, "Student") Student;
(5)    d_Ref<Student> temp_student =
                          new(d_Database::transient_memory, "Student") Student;
```

Statement (1) creates a transient object temp_sched1. Statements (2)–(4) create persistent objects. Statement (2) creates a new instance of class Professor in the database yourDB. Statement (3) creates a new instance of class Student in the database myDB. Statement (4) does the same thing, except that it specifies that the new object, student2, should be placed close to student1. Statement (5) creates a transient object temp_student.

5.3.1.1 Object Deletion

Objects, once created, can be deleted in C++ OML using the d_Ref::delete_object member function. Using the delete operator on a pointer to a persistent object will also delete the object, as in standard C++ practice. Deleting an object is permanent, subject to transaction commit. The object is removed from memory and, if it is a persistent object, from the database. The d_Ref instance or pointer still exists in memory but its reference value is undefined. An attempt to access the deleted object is implementation defined.

Example:

```
 d_Ref<anyType> obj_ref;
 ...   // set obj_ref to refer to a persistent object
 obj_ref.delete_object();
```

C++ requires the operand of delete to be a pointer, so the member function delete_object was defined to delete an object with just a d_Ref<T> reference to it.

5.3.1.2 Object Modification

The state of an object is modified by updating its properties or by invoking operations on it. Updates to persistent objects are made visible to other users of the database when the transaction containing the modifications commits.

Persistent objects that will be modified must communicate to the runtime ODBMS process the fact that their states will change. The ODBMS will then update the database with these new states at transaction commit time. Object change is communicated by invoking the d_Object::mark_modified member function, which is defined in Section 5.3.4 and is used as follows:

```
obj_ref->mark_modified();
```

The mark_modified function call is included in the constructor and destructor methods for persistence-capable classes, i.e., within class d_Object. The developer should include the call in any other methods that modify persistent objects, before the object is actually modified.

As a convenience, the programmer may omit calls to mark_modified on objects where classes have been compiled using an optional C++ OML preprocessor switch; the system will automatically detect when the objects are modified. In the default case, mark_modified calls are required, because in some ODMG implementations performance will be better when the programmer explicitly calls mark_modified. However, each time a persistent object is modified by a member update function provided explicitly by the ODMG classes, the mark_modified call is not necessary since it is done automatically.

5.3.1.3 Object References

Objects, whether persistent or not, may refer to other objects via object references. In C++ OML object references are instances of the template class d_Ref<T> (see Section 5.3.5). All accesses to persistent objects are made via methods defined on classes d_Ref, d_Object, and d_Database. The dereference operator –> is used to access members of the persistent object "addressed" by a given object reference. How an object reference is converted to a C++ pointer to the object is implementation-defined.

A dereference operation on an object reference always guarantees that the object referred to is returned or a d_Error exception object of kind d_Error_RefInvalid is thrown. The behavior of a reference is as follows. If an object reference refers to a persistent object that exists but is not in memory when a dereference is performed, it will be retrieved automatically from disk, mapped into memory and returned as the result of the dereference. If the referenced object does not exist, a d_Error exception object of kind d_Error_RefInvalid is thrown. References to transient objects work exactly the same (at least on the surface) as references to persistent objects.

Any object reference may be set to a null reference or *cleared* to indicate the reference does not refer to an object.

The rules for when an object of one lifetime may refer to an object of another lifetime are a straightforward extension of the C++ rules for its two forms of transient objects — procedure coterminus and process coterminus. An object can always refer to another object of longer lifetime. An object can only refer to an object of shorter lifetime as long as the shorter-lived object exists.

A persistent object is retrieved from disk upon activation. It is the application's responsibility to initialize the values of any of that object's pointers to transient objects. When a persistent object is committed, the ODBMS sets its embedded d_Refs to transient objects to the null value.

5.3.1.4 Object Names

A database application generally will begin processing by accessing one or more critical objects and proceeding from there. These objects are in some sense "root" objects, in that they lead to interconnected webs of other objects. The ability to name an object and retrieve it later by that name facilitates this start-up capability. Named objects are also convenient in many other situations.

There is a single, flat name scope per database; thus all names in a particular database are unique. A name is not explicitly defined as an attribute of an object. The operations for manipulating names are defined in the d_Database class in Section 5.3.8.

5.3.2 Properties

5.3.2.1 Attributes

C++ OML uses standard C++ for accessing attributes. For example, assume prof has been initialized to reference a professor and we wish to modify its id_number:

```
prof->id_number = next_id;
cout << prof->id_number;
```

Modifying an attribute's value is considered a modification to the enclosing object instance. One must call mark_modified for the object before it is modified.

The C++ binding allows persistence-capable classes to embed instances of C++ classes, including other persistence-capable classes. However, embedded objects are not considered "independent objects" and have no object identity of their own. Users are not permitted to get a d_Ref to an embedded object. Just as with any attribute, modifying an embedded object is considered a modification to the enclosing object instance, and mark_modified for the enclosing object must be called before the embedded object is modified.

5.3.2.2 Relationships

The ODL specifies which relationships exist between object classes. Creating, traversing, and breaking relationships between instances are defined in the C++ OML. Both to-one and to-many traversal paths are supported by the OML. The integrity of relationships is maintained by the ODBMS.

The following diagrams will show graphically the effect of adding, modifying, and deleting relationships among classes. Each diagram is given a name to reflect the cardinality and resulting effect on the relationship. The name will begin with 1-1, 1-m or m-m to denote the cardinality and will end in either N (No relationship), A (Add a relationship) or M (Modify a relationship). When a relationship is deleted, this will result in a state of having no relationship (N). A solid line is drawn to denote the explicit operation performed by the program and a dashed line shows the side effect operation performed automatically by the ODBMS to maintain referential integrity.

The following template class allows one to specify a to-one relationship to a class T.

```
template <class T, const char *Member> class d_Rel_Ref : public d_Ref<T> { };
```

The template d_Rel_Ref<T,M> supports the same interface as d_Ref<T>. Implementations will redefine some functions to provide support for referential integrity.

The application programmer must introduce two const char * variables, one used at each end of the relationship to refer to the other end of the relationship, thus establishing the association of the two ends of the relationship. The variables must be initialized with the name of the attribute at the other end of the relationship.

Assume the following 1-1 relationship exists between class A and class B:

```
extern const char _ra [ ], _rb [ ] ;
class A {
    d_Rel_Ref<B, _ra>    rb;
};
class B {
    d_Rel_Ref<A, _rb>    ra;
};
const char _ra [ ] = "ra";
const char _rb [ ] = "rb";
```

Note that class A and B could be the same class, as well. In each of the diagrams below, there will be an instance of A called a or aa and an instance of B called b or bb. In the following scenario 1-1N there is no relationship between a and b.

1-1N: No relationship

Then, adding a relationship between a and b via

        a.rb = &b;

results in the following:

1-1A: Add a relationship

The solid arrow indicates the operation specified by the program and the dashed line shows what operation gets performed automatically by the ODBMS.

Assume now the previous diagram (1-1A) represents the current state of the relationship between a and b. If the program executes the statement

        a.rb.clear ();

the result will be no relationship as shown in 1-1N.

Assume we have the relationship depicted in 1-1A. If we now execute

        a.rb = &bb;

we obtain the following:

1-1M: Modify relationship

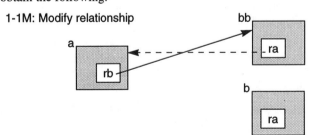

Notice that b.ra no longer refers to A and bb.ra is set automatically to reference a.

Whenever the operand to initialization or assignment represents a null reference, the result will be no relationship as in 1-1N. In the case of assignment, if there had been a relationship, it is removed. If the relationship is currently null (is_null would return true), then doing an assignment would add a relationship, unless the assignment operand was null as well.

If there is currently a relationship with an object, then doing the assignment will modify the relationship as in 1-1M. If the assignment operand is null, then the existing relationship is removed.

When an object involved in a relationship is deleted, all the relationships that the object was involved in will be removed as well.

There are two other cardinalities to consider: one-to-many and many-to-many. With one-to-many and many-to-many relationships, the set of operations allowed are based upon whether the relationship is an unordered set or positional.

The following template class allows one to specify an unordered to-many relationship with a class T.

```
template <class T, const char *M> class d_Rel_Set : public d_Set<d_Ref<T> > { }
```

The template d_Rel_Set<T,M> supports the same interface as d_Set<d_Ref<T> >. Implementations will redefine some functions in order to support referential integrity.

Assuming an unordered one-to-many set relationship between class A and class B:

```
extern const char _ra [ ], _sb [ ] ;


class A {
    d_Rel_Set<B, _ra>    sb;
};
class B {
    d_Rel_Ref<A, _sb>    ra;
};
const char _ra[ ] = "ra";
const char _sb[ ] = "sb";
```

Assume we have the following instances a and b with no relationship.

1-mN: No relationship

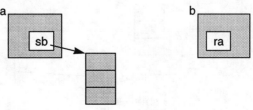

a.sb has 3 elements, but they are referring to instances of B other than b.

Now suppose we add a relationship between **a** and **b** by executing the statement

      a.sb.insert_element (&b);

This results in the following:

   1-mA: Add a relationship

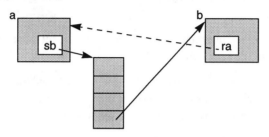

The b.ra traversal path gets set automatically to reference **a**. Conversely, if we execute
the statement

      b.ra = &a;

an element would have automatically been added to **a.sb** to refer to **b**. But only one of
the two operations needs to be performed by the program, the ODBMS automatically
updates the inverse traversal path.

Given the situation depicted in 1-mA, if we execute either

      a.sb.remove_element (&b)   or   b.ra.clear ();

the result would be that the relationship between **a** and **b** would be deleted and the state
of **a** and **b** would be as depicted in 1-mN.

Now assume we have the relationship between **a** and **b** as shown in 1-mA. If we
execute the following statement:

      b.ra = &aa;

this results in the following:

   1-mM: Modify a relationship

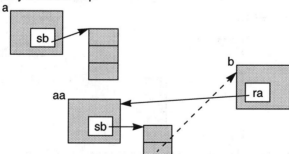

After the statement executes, b.ra refers to aa, and as a side effect, the element within a.sb that had referred to b is removed and an element is added to aa.sb to refer to b.

The d_List class represents a *positional* collection, whereas the d_Set class is an unordered collection. Likewise, the d_Rel_List<T, Member> template is used for representing relationships which are positional in nature.

```
template <class T, const char *M> class d_Rel_List : public d_List<d_Ref<T> > { };
```

The template d_Rel_List<T,M> has the same interface as d_List<d_Ref<T> >.

Assuming a positional to-many relationship between class A and class B:

```
extern const char _ra [ ] , _listB [ ] ;


class A {
     d_Rel_List<B, _ra>          listB;
};
class B {
     d_Rel_Ref<A, _listB>        ra;
};
const char _ra [ ] = "ra";
const char _listB [ ] = "listB";
```

The third relationship cardinality to consider is many-to-many. Suppose we have the following relationship between A and B.

```
extern const char _sa [ ], _sb [ ] ;


class A {
     d_Rel_Set<B, _sa>    sb;
};
class B {
     d_Rel_Set<A, _sb>    sa;
};
const char _sa [ ] = "sa";
const char _sb [ ] = "sb";
```

Initially, there will be no relationship between instances a and b though a and b have relationships with other instances.

m-mN: No relationship

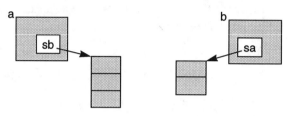

The following statement will add a relationship between a and b.

a.sb.insert_element (&b);

This will result in the following:

m-mA: Add a relationship

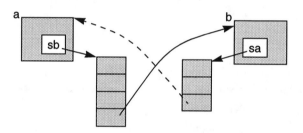

In addition to an element being added to **a.sb** to reference b, there is an element automatically added to **b.sa** that references **a**.

Executing either

a.sb.remove_element(&b)   or   b.sa.remove_element(&a)

would result in the relationship being removed between a and b, and the result would be as depicted in m-mN.

Last, we consider the modification of a many-to-many relationship. Assume the prior state is the situation depicted in m-mA, and assume that sb represents a positional relationship. The following statement will modify an existing relationship that exists between a and b, changing a to be related to bb.

a.sb.replace_element_at(&bb, 3);

This results in the following object relationships:

m-mM: Modify a relationship

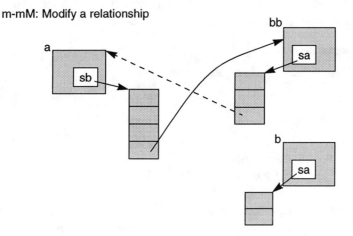

The result of this operation is that the element in b.sa that referenced a is removed and an element is added to bb.sa to reference a.

The initializations and assignments which have an argument of type d_Rel_Set<T,Member> or d_Set<d_Ref<T> > are much more involved than the simple diagrams above because they involve performing the corresponding operation for every element of the set versus doing it for just one element. The remove_all function removes every member of the relationship also removing the back-reference for each referenced member. If the assignment operators have an argument that represents an empty set, the assignment will have the same effect as the remove_all function.

Below are some more examples based on the classes used throughout the chapter.

Examples:

```
d_Ref<Professor> p;
d_Ref<Student> Sam;
d_Ref<Department> english_dept;
// initialize p, Sam, and english_dept references
p->dept = english_dept;   // create 1:1 relationship
p->dept.clear();              // clear the relationship
p->advisees.insert_element(Sam); // add Sam to the set of students that are p's
                                 // advisees; same effect as 'Sam->advisor = p'
p->advisees.remove_element(Sam); // remove Sam from the set of students that
                                 // are p's advisees, also clears Sam->advisor
```

5.3.3 Operations

Operations are defined in the OML as they are generally implemented in C++. Operations on transient and persistent objects behave entirely consistently with the operational context defined by standard C++. This includes all overloading, dispatching, function call structure and invocation, member function call structure and invocation, argument passing and resolution, error handling, and compile time rules.

5.3.4 d_Object Class

The class d_Object is introduced and defined as follows:

Definition:

```
class  d_Object {
public:
                        d_Object();
                        d_Object(const d_Object &);
virtual                 ~d_Object();
    d_Object &          operator=(const d_Object &);
    void                mark_modified();  // mark the object as modified
    void *              operator new(size_t size);
    void *              operator new(size_t size, const d_Ref_Any &cluster,
                                  const char *typename);
    void *              operator new(size_t size, d_Database *database,
                                  const char *typename);
    void                operator delete(void *);
virtual    void         d_activate();
virtual    void         d_deactivate();
};
```

This class is introduced to allow the type definer to specify when a class is capable of having persistent as well as transient instances. Instances of classes derived from d_Object can be either persistent or transient. A class A that is persistence-capable would inherit from class d_Object:

```
    class My_Class : public d_Object {...};
```

Some implementations, although they accept the d_Object superclass as an indication of potential persistence, need not physically introduce a d_Object class. All implementations accept the mark_modified call, even if the d_Object class does not exist.

The delete operator can be used with a pointer to a persistent object to delete the object; the object is removed from both the application cache and the database, which is the same behavior as Ref<T>::delete_object.

An application needs to initialize and manage the transient members of a persistent object as the object enters and exits the application cache. Memory may need to be allocated and deallocated when these events occur, for example. The d_activate function is called when an object enters the application cache, and d_deactivate is called when the object exits the application cache. Normally C++ code uses the constructor and destructor to perform initialization and destruction, but in an ODMG implementation the constructor only gets called when an object is first created and the destructor is called at the point the object is deleted from the database. The following diagram depicts the calls made throughout the lifetime of an object.

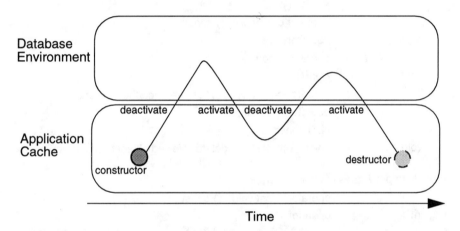

The object first gets initialized by the constructor. At the point the object exits the application cache, the d_deactivate function gets called. When the object re-enters the application cache, d_activate gets called. This may get repeated many times, as the object moves in and out of an application cache. Eventually, the object gets deleted, in which case only the destructor gets called, not d_deactivate.

5.3.5 Reference Classes

Objects may refer to other objects through a smart pointer or reference called a d_Ref. A d_Ref<T> is a reference to an instance of type T. There is also a d_Ref_Any class defined that provides a generic reference to any type.

A d_Ref is a template class defined as follows:

Definition:

```
template <class T> class d_Ref {
public:
                    d_Ref();
                    d_Ref(T *fromPtr );
                    d_Ref(const d_Ref<T> &);
                    d_Ref(const d_Ref_Any &);
                    ~d_Ref();
                    operator d_Ref_Any() const;
d_Ref<T> &          operator=(T *);
d_Ref<T> &          operator=(const d_Ref<T>&);
void                clear();
T *                 operator->() const;     // dereference the reference
T &                 operator*() const;
T *                 ptr() const;
void                delete_object();  // delete referred object from memory
                                      // and the database
// boolean predicates to check reference
                    operator const void *() const;
int                 operator!() const;
int                 is_null() const;
// do these d_Refs and pointers refer to the same objects?
friend  int         operator==(const d_Ref<T> &refL, const d_Ref<T> &refR );
friend  int         operator==(const d_Ref<T> &refL, const T *ptrR );
friend  int         operator==(const T *ptrL, const d_Ref<T> &refR );
friend  int         operator==(const d_Ref<T> &L, const d_Ref_Any &R);
friend  int         operator==(const d_Ref_Any &L, const d_Ref<T> &R);
friend  int         operator!=( const d_Ref<T> &refL, const d_Ref<T> &refR );
friend  int         operator!=( const d_Ref<T> &refL, const T *ptrR );
friend  int         operator!=( const T *ptrL, const d_Ref<T> &refR );
friend  int         operator!=( const d_Ref<T> &refL, const d_Ref_Any &anyR);
friend  int         operator!=( const d_Ref_Any &anyL, const d_Ref<T> &refR);
};
```

References in many respects behave like C++ pointers but provide an additional mechanism that guarantees integrity in references to persistent objects. Although the syntax for declaring a d_Ref is different than for declaring a pointer, the usage is, in most cases, the same due to overloading; e.g., d_Refs may be dereferenced with the * operator, assigned with the = operator, etc. A d_Ref to a class may be assigned to a d_Ref to a superclass. d_Refs may be sub-classed to provide specific referencing behavior.

There is one anomaly that results from the ability to do conversions between d_Ref<T> and d_Ref_Any. The following code will compile without error, and a d_Error exception object of kind d_Error_TypeInvalid is thrown at run-time versus statically at compile time. Suppose that X and Y are two unrelated classes.

```
d_Ref<X>   x;
d_Ref<Y>   y(x);
```

The initialization of y via x will be done via a conversion to d_Ref_Any. One should avoid such initializations in their application.

The pointer or reference returned by operator–> or operator * is only valid until either the d_Ref is deleted, the end of the outermost transaction, or until the object it points to is deleted. The pointer returned by ptr is only valid until the end of the outermost transaction or until the object it points to is deleted. The value of a d_Ref after a transaction commit or abort is undefined. If an attempt is made to dereference a null d_Ref<T>, a d_Error exception object of kind d_Error_RefNull is thrown.

The following template class allows one to specify a to-one relationship to a class T.

```
template <class T, const char *Member> class d_Rel_Ref : public d_Ref<T> { };
```

The template d_Rel_Ref<T,M> supports the same interface as d_Ref<T>. Implementations will redefine some functions to provide support for referential integrity.

A class d_Ref_Any is defined to support a reference to any type. Its primary purpose is to handle generic references and allow conversions of d_Refs in the type hierarchy. A d_Ref_Any object can be used as an intermediary between any two types d_Ref<X> and d_Ref<Y> where X and Y are different types. A d_Ref<T> can always be converted to a d_Ref_Any; there is a function to perform the conversion in the d_Ref<T> template. Each d_Ref<T> class has a constructor and assignment operator that takes a reference to a d_Ref_Any.

The d_Ref_Any class is defined as follows:

Definition:

```
class d_Ref_Any {
public:
                    d_Ref_Any();
                    d_Ref_Any(const d_Ref_Any &);
                    d_Ref_Any(d_Object *);
                    ~d_Ref_Any();
    d_Ref_Any &     operator=(const d_Ref_Any &);
```

```
d_Ref_Any &       operator=(d_Object *);
void              clear();
void              delete_object();

// boolean predicates checking to see if value is null or not
                  operator const void *() const;
int               operator!() const;
int               is_null() const;

friend  int       operator==(const d_Ref_Any &, const d_Ref_Any &);
friend  int       operator==(const d_Ref_Any &, const d_Object *);
friend  int       operator==(const d_Object *, const d_Ref_Any &);
friend  int       operator!=(const d_Ref_Any &, const d_Ref_Any &);
friend  int       operator!=(const d_Ref_Any &, const d_Object *);
friend  int       operator!=(const d_Object *, const d_Ref_Any &);
};
```

The operations defined on d_Ref<T> that are not dependent on a specific type T have been provided in the d_Ref_Any class.

5.3.6 Collection Classes

Collection templates are provided to support the representation of a collection whose elements are of an arbitrary type. A conforming implementation must support at least the following subtypes of d_Collection:

- d_Set
- d_Bag
- d_List
- d_Varray

The C++ class definitions for each of these types are defined in the subsections that follow. Iterators are defined as a final subsection.

The following discussion uses the d_Set class in its explanation of collections, but the description applies for all concrete classes derived from d_Collection.

Given an object of type T, the declaration

```
d_Set<T> s;
```

defines a d_Set collection whose elements are of type T. If this set is assigned to another set of the same type, both the d_Set object itself and each of the elements of the set are copied. The elements are copied using the copy semantics defined for the type T. A common convention will be to have a collection that contains d_Refs to persistent objects. For example,

```
d_Set<d_Ref<Professor> > faculty;
```

The d_Ref class has shallow copy semantics. For a d_Set<T>, if T is of type d_Ref<C>
for some persistent class C, only the d_Ref objects are copied, not the C objects that
the d_Ref objects reference.

This holds in any scope; in particular, if s is declared as a member inside a class, the
set itself will be embedded inside an instance of this class. When an object of this
enclosing class is copied into another object of the same enclosing class, the embedded
set is copied, too, following the copy semantics defined above. This must be differen-
tiated from the declaration

    d_Ref<d_Set<T> > ref_set;

which defines a reference to a d_Set. When such a reference is defined as a property
of a class, that means that the set itself is an independent object which lies outside an
instance of the enclosing class. Several objects may then share the same set, since
copying an object will not copy the set, but just the reference to it. These are illustrated
in Figure 5-2.

Collection elements may be of any type. Every type T that will become an element of
a given collection must support the following operations:

```
class T {
public:
                T();
                T(const T &);
                ~T();
        T &     operator=(const T &);
    friend int  operator==(const T&, const T&);
};
```

This is the complete set of functions required for defining the copy semantics for a
given type. For types requiring ordering, the following operation must also be
provided:

```
    friend int  operator<(const T&, const T&);
```

Note that the C++ compiler will automatically generate a copy constructor and assignment operator if the class designer does not declare one. Note that the d_Ref<T> class
supports these operations, except for operator<.

Collections of literals, including both atomic and structured literals, are defined as part
of the standard. This includes both primitive and user-defined types; e.g., d_Set<int>,
d_Set<struct time_t> will be defined with the same behavior.

Figure 5-2 illustrates various types involving d_Sets, d_Refs, a literal type L (int for
example) and a persistent class T. The d_Set object itself is represented by a box that
then refers to a set of elements of the specified type. A solid arrow is used to denote

containment of the set elements within the d_Set object. d_Refs have a dashed arrow
pointing to the referenced object of type T.

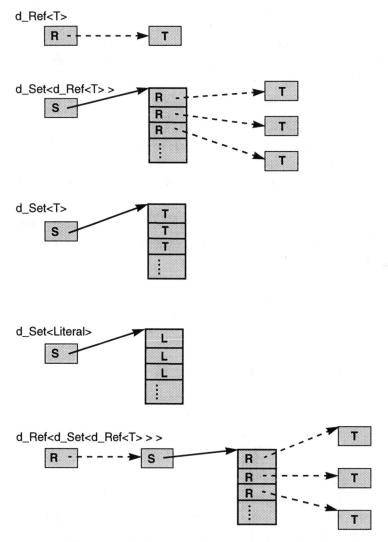

Figure 5-2. Collections, Embedded and with d_Ref

5.3.6.1 Class d_Collection

Class d_Collection is an abstract class in C++ and cannot have instances. It is derived
from d_Object, allowing instances of concrete classes derived from d_Collection to be
stand-alone persistent objects. It is also the case as is discussed in Section 5.3.4 on
d_Object that not all implementations require that the d_Object class be introduced to

support persistence; these implementations will not necessarily derive d_Collection from d_Object.

Definition:

```
template <class T> class d_Collection : public d_Object {
public:
virtual               ~d_Collection();
    d_Collection<T> &assign_from(const d_Collection<T> &);
friend  int           operator==(  const d_Collection<T> &cL,
                                   const d_Collection<T> &cR);
friend  int           operator!=(  const d_Collection<T> &cL,
                                   const d_Collection<T> &cR);
    unsigned long     cardinality() const;
    int               is_empty() const;
    int               is_ordered() const;
    int               allows_duplicates() const;
    int               contains_element(const T &element) const;
    void              insert_element(const T &elem);
    void              remove_element(const T &elem);
    void              remove_all();
    d_Iterator<T>     create_iterator() const;
    d_Iterator<T>     begin() const;
    d_Iterator<T>     end() const;
    const T &         select_element(const char *OQL_predicate) const;
    d_Iterator<T>     select(const char * OQL_predicate) const;
    int               query(d_Collection<T> &, const char *OQL_pred) const;
    int               exists_element(const char* OQL_predicate) const;
protected:
                d_Collection(const d_Collection<T> &);
    d_Collection<T> &operator=(const d_Collection<T> &);
                d_Collection();
};
```

Note that the d_Collection class provides the operation assign_from in place of operator= because d_Collection assignment is relatively expensive. This will prevent the often gratuitous use of assignment with collections.

The create_iterator function returns an iterator pointing at the first element in the collection. The begin and end functions are supplied for compatibility with the C++ Standard Template Library (STL) algorithms. As defined in STL, the "past end" iterator value returned by the end function is not dereferenceable.

5.3.6.2 Class d_Set

A d_Set<T> is an unordered collection of elements of type T with no duplicates.

Definition:

```
template <class T> class d_Set : public d_Collection<T> {
public:
                        d_Set();
                        d_Set(const d_Set<T> &);
                        ~d_Set();
    d_Set<T> &          operator=(const d_Set<T> &);
    d_Set<T> &          union_of(const d_Set<T> &sL, const d_Set<T> &sR);
    d_Set<T> &          union_with(const d_Set<T> &s2);
    d_Set<T> &          operator+=(const d_Set<T> &s2);        // union_with
    d_Set<T>            create_union(const d_Set<T> &s) const;
    friend  d_Set<T>    operator+(const d_Set<T> &s1, const d_Set<T> &s2);
    d_Set<T> &          intersection_of(const d_Set<T> &sL, const d_Set<T> &sR);
    d_Set<T> &          intersection_with(const d_Set<T> &s2);
    d_Set<T> &          operator*=(const d_Set<T> &s2);        // intersection_with
    d_Set<T>            create_intersection(const d_Set<T> &s) const;
    friend  d_Set<T>    operator*(const d_Set<T> &s1, const d_Set<T> &s2);
    d_Set<T> &          difference_of(const d_Set<T> &sL, const d_Set<T> &sR);
    d_Set<T> &          difference_with(const d_Set<T> &s2);
    d_Set<T> &          operator-=(const d_Set<T> &s2);        // difference_with
    d_Set<T>            create_difference(const d_Set<T> &s) const;
    friend  d_Set<T>    operator-(const d_Set<T> &s1, const d_Set<T> &s2);
    int                 is_subset_of(const d_Set<T> &s2) const;
    int                 is_proper_subset_of(const  d_Set<T> &s2) const;
    int                 is_superset_of(const d_Set<T> &s2) const;
    int                 is_proper_superset_of(const d_Set<T> &s2) const;
};
```

Note that all operations defined on type d_Collection are inherited by type d_Set, e.g., insert_element, remove_element, select_element, and select.

Examples:

- creation:
  ```
  d_Database db;              // assume we open a database
  d_Ref<Professor> Guttag; // assume we set this to a professor
  d_Ref<d_Set<d_Ref<Professor> > > my_profs =
                          new(&db) d_Set<d_Ref<Professor> >;
  ```

- insertion:
  my_profs–>insert_element(Guttag);

- removal:
  my_profs–>remove_element(Guttag);

- deletion:
  my_profs.delete_object();

For each of the set operations (union, intersection, and difference) there are three ways of computing the resulting set. These will be explained using the union operation. Each one of the union functions has two set operands and computes their union. They vary in how the set operands are passed and how the result is returned, to support different interface styles. The union_of function is a member function that has two arguments which are references to d_Set<T>. It computes the union of the two sets and places the result in the d_Set object with which the function was called, removing the original contents of the set. The union_with function is also a member and places its result in the object with which the operation is invoked, removing its original contents. The difference is that union_with uses its current set contents as one of the two operands being unioned, thus requiring only one operand passed to the member function. Both union_of and union_with return a reference to the object with which the operation was invoked. The union_with function has a corresponding operator+= function defined. On the other hand, create_union creates and returns a new d_Set instance by value that contains the union, leaving the two original sets unaltered. This function also has a corresponding operator+ function defined.

The following template class allows one to specify an unordered to-many relationship with a class T.

```
template <class T, const char *M> class d_Rel_Set : public d_Set<d_Ref<T> > { }
```

The template d_Rel_Set<T,M> supports the same interface as d_Set<d_Ref<T> >. Implementations will redefine some functions in order to support referential integrity.

5.3.6.3 Class d_Bag

A d_Bag<T> is an unordered collection of elements of type T that does allow for duplicate values.

Definition:

```
template <class T> class d_Bag : public d_Collection<T> {
public:
                    d_Bag();
                    d_Bag(const d_Bag<T> &);
                    ~d_Bag();
```

```
       d_Bag<T> &      operator=(const d_Bag<T> &);
       d_Bag<T> &      union_of(const d_Bag<T> &bL, const d_Bag<T> &bR);
       d_Bag<T> &      union_with(const d_Bag<T> &b2);
       d_Bag<T> &      operator+=(const d_Bag<T> &b2); // union_with
       d_Bag<T>        create_union(const d_Bag<T> &b) const;
 friend d_Bag<T>       operator+(const d_Bag<T> &b1, const d_Bag<T> &b2);
       d_Bag<T> &      intersection_of(const d_Bag<T> &bL, const d_Bag<T> &bR);
       d_Bag<T> &      intersection_with(const d_Bag<T> &b2);
       d_Bag<T> &      operator*=(const d_Bag<T> &b2);   // intersection_with
       d_Bag<T>        create_intersection(const d_Bag<T>&b) const;
 friend d_Bag<T>       operator*(const d_Bag<T> &b1, const d_Bag<T> &b2);
       d_Bag<T> &      difference_of(const d_Bag<T> &bL, const d_Bag<T> &bR);
       d_Bag<T> &      difference_with(const d_Bag<T> &b2);
       d_Bag<T> &      operator-=(const d_Bag<T> &b2); // difference_with
       d_Bag<T>        create_difference(const d_Bag<T> &b) const;
 friend d_Bag<T>       operator-(const d_Bag<T> &b1, const d_Bag<T> &b2);
};
```

The union, intersection, and difference operations are described in the section above on the d_Set class.

5.3.6.4 Class d_List

A d_List<T> is an ordered collection of elements of type T and does allow for duplicate values. The beginning d_List index value is 0, following the convention of C and C++.

Definition:

```
template <class T> class d_List : public d_Collection<T> {
public:
                   d_List ();
                   d_List(const d_List<T> &);
                   ~d_List ();
       d_List<T> & operator=(const d_List<T> &);
       const T &   retrieve_first_element() const;
       const T &   retrieve_last_element() const;
       void        remove_first_element();
       void        remove_last_element();
       const T &   operator[ ](unsigned long position) const;
       int         find_element(const T &element,
                               unsigned long &position) const;
       const T &   retrieve_element_at(unsigned long position) const;
       void        remove_element_at(unsigned long position);
```

void	replace_element_at(const T &element, unsigned long position);
void	insert_element_first(const T &element);
void	insert_element_last(const T &element);
void	insert_element_after(const T & element, unsigned long position);
void	insert_element_before(const T &element, unsigned long position);
d_List<T>	concat(const d_List<T> &listR) const;
friend d_List<T>	operator+(const d_List<T> &listL, const d_List<T> &listR);
d_List<T> &	append(const d_List<T> &listR);
d_List<T> &	operator+=(const d_List<T> &listR);

```
};
```

The insert_element function (inherited from d_Collection <T>) inserts a new element at the end of the list.

The d_Rel_List<T, Member> template is used for representing relationships which are positional in nature.

```
template <class T, const char *M> class d_Rel_List : public d_List<d_Ref<T> > { };
```

The template d_Rel_List<T,M> has the same interface as d_List<d_Ref<T> >.

5.3.6.5 Class Array

The Array type defined in Section 2.3.1 is implemented by the built-in array defined by the C++ language. This is a single-dimension, fixed-length array.

5.3.6.6 Class d_Varray

A d_Varray<T> is a one-dimensional array of varying length containing elements of type T. The beginning d_Varray index value is 0, following the convention of C and C++.

Definition:

```
template <class T> class d_Varray : public d_Collection<T> {
public:
                    d_Varray();
                    d_Varray(unsigned long length);
                    d_Varray(const d_Varray<T> &);
                    ~d_Varray();
d_Varray<T> &       operator=(const d_Varray<T> &);
unsigned long       upper_bound() const;
void                resize(unsigned long length);
const T &           operator[](unsigned long index) const;
```

```
        int             find_element(const T &element,
                                    unsigned long &index ) const;
        const T &       retrieve_element_at(unsigned long index) const;
        void            remove_element_at(unsigned long index);
        void            replace_element_at(const T &element,
                                    unsigned long index);
};
```

The insert_element function (inherited from d_Collection <T>) inserts a new element by increasing the d_Varray length by one and placing the new element at this new position in the d_Varray.

Examples:

```
d_Varray<d_Double>  vector(1000);
vector.replace_element_at( 3.14159, 97);
vector.resize(2000);
```

5.3.6.7 Class d_Iterator

A template class, d_Iterator<T>, defines the generic behavior for iteration. All iterators use a consistent protocol for sequentially returning each element from the collection over which the iteration is defined. A template class has been used to give us type-safe iterators, i.e., iterators that are guaranteed to return an instance of the type of the element of the collection over which the iterator is defined. Normally, an iterator is initialized by the create_iterator method on a collection class.

The template class d_Iterator<T> is defined as follows:

```
template <class T> class d_Iterator {
public:
                        d_Iterator();
                        d_Iterator(const d_Iterator<T> &);
                        ~d_Iterator();
    d_Iterator<T> &     operator=(const d_Iterator<T> &);
    friend  int         operator==(const d_Iterator<T> &, const d_Iterator<T> &);
    friend  int         operator!=(const d_Iterator<T> &, const d_Iterator<T> &);
        void            reset();
        int             not_done() const;
        void            advance();
    d_Iterator<T> &     operator++();
    d_Iterator<T>       operator++(int);
    d_Iterator<T> &     operator--();
    d_Iterator<T>       operator--(int);
        T               get_element() const;
```

```
    T                    operator*() const;
    void                 replace_element(const T &);
    int                  next(T &objRef);
};
```

When an iterator is constructed, it is either initialized with another iterator or is set to null. When an iterator is constructed via the create_iterator function defined in d_Collection, the iterator is initialized to point to the first element, if there is one. Iterator assignment is also supported. A reset function is provided to re-initialize the iterator to the start of iteration for the same collection. The replace_element function can only be used with d_List or d_Varray.

The not_done function allows one to determine whether there are any more elements in the collection to be visited in the iteration. It returns 1 if there are more elements and 0 if iteration is complete. The advance function moves the iterator forward to the next element in the collection. The prefix and postfix forms of the increment operator ++ have been overloaded to provide an equivalent advance operation. One can also move backwards through the collection by using the decrement operator --. If an attempt is made to either advance an iterator once it has already reached the end of a collection or move backwards once the first element has been reached, a d_Error exception object of kind d_Error_IteratorExhausted is thrown.

The get_element function and operator* return the value of the current element. If there is no current element, a d_Error exception object of kind d_Error_IteratorExhausted is thrown. There would be no current element if iteration had been completed (not_done return of 0) or if the collection had no elements.

The next function provides a facility for checking the end of iteration, advancing the iterator and returning the current element, if there is one. Its behavior is as follows:

```
template <class T> int d_Iterator<T>::next(T &objRef)
{
    if( !not_done() ) return 0;   // no more elements, return false
    objRef = get_element();       // assign current element into output parameter
    advance();                    // advance to the next element
    return 1;                     // return true, that there is a next element
}
```

These operations allow for two styles of iteration, using either a while or for loop.

Example:

Given the class Student, with extent students:

```
(1)  d_Iterator<d_Ref<Student> > iter = students.create_iterator();
     d_Ref<Student> s;
```

```
(2)  while( iter.next(s) ) {

       ....

     }
```

Note that calling get_element after calling next will return a different element (the next element, if there is one). This is due to the fact that next will access the current element and then advance the iterator before returning.

Or equivalently with a for loop:

```
(3)  d_Iterator<d_Ref<Student> > iter = students.create_iterator();
(4)  for( ; iter.not_done(); iter++) {
(5)       d_Ref<Student> s = iter.get_element();

          ....

     }
```

Statement (1) defines an iterator iter that ranges over the collection students. Statement (2) iterates through this collection, returning a d_Ref to a Student on each successive call to next, binding it to the loop variable s. The body of the while statement is then executed once for each student in the collection students. In the for loop (3) the iterator is initialized, iteration is checked for completion, and the iterator is advanced. Inside the for loop the get_element function can be called to get the current element.

5.3.6.8 Collections and the Standard Template Library

The C++ Standard Template Library (STL) may be used to operate on the collection classes defined in the C++ OML. STL algorithms traverse container data structures using iterator objects, which are compatible with the d_Iterator<T> objects defined in the C++ OML. Specifically, d_Iterator<T> objects conform to the STL specification of constant iterators of category bidirectional_iterator, though an implementation may provide more powerful iterators in some circumstances.

5.3.7 Transactions

Transaction semantics are defined in the object model explained in Chapter 2.

Transactions can be started, committed, aborted, and checkpointed. It is important to note that *all access, creation, modification, and deletion of persistent objects must be done within a transaction.*

Transactions are implemented in C++ as objects of class d_Transaction. The class d_Transaction defines the operation for starting, committing, aborting, and check-pointing transactions. These operations are

```
class d_Transaction {
public:
                    d_Transaction();
                    ~d_Transaction();
```

```
        void            begin();
        void            commit();
        void            abort();
        void            checkpoint();
private:
                        d_Transaction(const d_Transaction &);
        d_Transaction & operator=(const d_Transaction &);
};
```

Transactions must be explicitly created and started; they are not automatically started on database open, upon creation of a d_Transaction object, nor following a transaction commit or abort.

The begin function starts a transaction. Calling begin multiple times on the same transaction object, without an intervening commit or abort, causes a d_Error exception object of kind d_Error_TransactionOpen to be thrown on second and subsequent calls.

Calling commit commits to the database all persistent objects modified (including those created or deleted) within the transaction and releases any locks held by the transaction. Implementations may choose to maintain the validity of d_Refs to persistent objects across transaction boundaries. The commit operation does not delete the transaction object.

Calling checkpoint commits objects modified within the transaction since the last checkpoint to the database. The transaction retains all locks it held on those objects at the time the checkpoint was invoked. All d_Refs and pointers remain unchanged.

Calling abort aborts changes to objects and releases the locks, and does not delete the transaction object.

The destructor aborts the transaction if it is active.

In the current standard, transient objects are not subject to transaction semantics. Committing a transaction does not remove transient objects from memory. Aborting a transaction does not restore the state of modified transient objects.

d_Transaction objects are not long-lived (beyond process boundaries) and cannot be stored to the database. This means that transaction objects may not be made persistent and that the notion of "long transactions" is not defined in this specification.

In summary the rules that apply to object modification (necessarily, during a transaction) are

1. Changes made to persistent objects within a transaction can be "undone" by aborting the transaction.

2. Transient objects are standard C++ objects.

3. Persistent objects created within the scope of a transaction are handled consistently at transaction boundaries: stored to the database and removed from memory (at transaction commit) or deleted (as a result of a transaction abort).

5.3.8 d_Database Operations

There is a predefined type d_Database. It supports the following methods:

```
class d_Database {
public:
static const d_Database * const transient_memory;
    enum access_status { not_open, read_write, read_only, exclusive };
    void             open(   const char * database_name,
                                 access_status status = read_write);
    void             close();
    void             set_object_name(const d_Ref_Any &theObject,
                                     const char* theName);
    void             rename_object(   const char * oldName,
                                     const char * newName);
    d_Ref_Any        lookup_object(const char * name) const;
private:
                     d_Database(const d_Database &);
    d_Database &     operator=(const d_Database &);
};
```

The database object, like the transaction object, is transient. Databases cannot be created programmatically using the C++ OML defined by this standard. Databases must be opened before starting any transactions which use the database, and closed after ending these transactions.

To open a database, use d_Database::open, which takes the name of the database as its argument. This initializes the instance of the d_Database object.

```
database–>open("myDB");
```

Method open locates the named database and makes the appropriate connection to the database. You must open a database before you can access objects in that database. Attempts to open a database when it has already been opened will result in the throwing of a d_Error exception object of kind d_Error_DatabaseOpen. Extensions to the open method will enable some ODBMSs to implement default database names and/or implicitly open a default database when a database session is started. Some ODBMSs may support opening logical as well as physical databases. Some ODBMSs may support being connected to multiple databases at the same time.

To close a database, use d_Database::close:

    database->close();

Method close does appropriate clean-up on the named database connection. After you have closed a database, further attempts to access objects in the database will cause a d_Error exception object of kind d_Error_DatabaseClosed to be thrown. The behavior at program termination if databases are not closed or transactions are not committed or aborted is undefined.

The *name* methods allow manipulating names of objects. An object can only acquire one name. The set_object_name method assigns a character string name to the object referenced. If the string supplied as the name argument is not unique within the database, a d_Error exception object of kind d_Error_NameNotUnique will be thrown. If the object already has a name, it is renamed to the new name. The rename_object method changes the name of an object. If the new name is already in use, a d_Error exception object of kind d_Error_NameNotUnique will be thrown and the old name is retained. A named object may have its name removed by providing 0 as the pointer value for the new name. When a named object is deleted, its name entry is automatically removed.

An object is accessed by name using the d_Database::lookup_object member function.

Example:

    d_Ref<Professor> prof = myDatabase->lookup_object("Newton");

If a Professor instance named "Newton" exists, it is retrieved and a d_Ref_Any is returned by lookup_object. The d_Ref_Any return value is then used to initialize prof. If the object named "Newton" is not an instance of Professor or a subclass of Professor, a d_Error exception object of kind d_Error_TypeInvalid is thrown during this initialization.

If the definition of a class in the application does not match the database definition of the class, a d_Error exception object of kind d_Error_DatabaseClassMismatch is thrown.

5.4 C++ OQL

Chapter 4 outlined the Object Query Language. In this section the OQL semantics are mapped into the C++ language. There are generally two options for binding a query sublanguage to a programming language: loosely coupled or tightly coupled. In the loosely coupled approach query functions are introduced that take strings containing queries as their arguments. These functions parse and evaluate the query at runtime, returning the result via the output parameter result. In the tightly coupled approach the query sublanguage is integrated directly into the programming language by expanding the definition of the nonterminals <term>, <expression> as defined in the BNF of the programming language. The tightly coupled approach allows queries to be optimized at compile time; in the loosely coupled approach they are generally optimized at execution time. The C++ binding for OQL supports the loosely coupled approach via a free-standing function called d_oql_execute.

5.4.1 d_oql_execute Function

An interface is provided to gain access to the complete functionality of OQL from a C++ program. There are several steps involved in the specification and execution of the OQL query. First, a query gets *constructed* via an object of type d_OQL_Query. Once a query has been constructed, the query is *executed*. Once constructed, a query can be executed multiple times with different argument values.

The function to execute a query is called d_oql_execute, it is a free-standing template function, not part of any class definition.

```
template<class T> void    d_oql_execute(d_OQL_Query &query, T &result);
```

The first parameter, *query*, is a reference to a d_OQL_Query object specifying the query to execute. The second parameter, *result*, is used for returning the result of the query. The type of the query result must match the type of this second parameter, or a d_Error exception object of kind d_Error_QueryParameterTypeInvalid is thrown. Type checking of the input parameters according to their use in the query is done at runtime. Similarly, the type of the result of the query is checked. Any violation of type would cause a d_Error exception object of kind d_Error_QueryParameterTypeInvalid to be thrown. If the query returns a persistent object of type T, the function returns a Ref<T>. If the query returns a structured literal, the value of it is assigned to the value of the object or collection denoted by the *result* parameter.

The << operator has been overloaded for d_OQL_Query to allow construction of the query. It concatenates the value of the right operand onto the end of the current value of the d_OQL_Query left operand. These functions return a reference to the left operand so that invocations can be cascaded.

Note that instances of d_OQL_Query contain either a partial or a complete OQL query. An ODMG implementation will contain ancillary data structures to represent a query both during its construction and once it is executed. The d_OQL_Query destructor will appropriately remove any ancillary data when the object gets deleted.

The d_OQL_Query class is defined as follows:

Definition:

```
class d_OQL_Query {
public:
                    d_OQL_Query();
                    d_OQL_Query(const char *s);
                    d_OQL_Query(const d_String &s);
                    d_OQL_Query(const d_OQL_Query &q);
                    ~d_OQL_Query();
    d_OQL_Query &  operator=(const d_OQL_Query &q);

    friend d_OQL_Query &operator<<(d_OQL_Query &q, const char *s);
    friend d_OQL_Query &operator<<(d_OQL_Query &q, const d_String &s);
    friend d_OQL_Query &operator<<(d_OQL_Query &q, d_Char c);
    friend d_OQL_Query &operator<<(d_OQL_Query &q, d_Octet uc);
    friend d_OQL_Query &operator<<(d_OQL_Query &q, d_Short s);
    friend d_OQL_Query &operator<<(d_OQL_Query &q, d_UShort us);
    friend d_OQL_Query &operator<<(d_OQL_Query &q, int i);
    friend d_OQL_Query &operator<<(d_OQL_Query &q, unsigned int ui);
    friend d_OQL_Query &operator<<(d_OQL_Query &q, d_Long l);
    friend d_OQL_Query &operator<<(d_OQL_Query &q, d_ULong ul);
    friend d_OQL_Query &operator<<(d_OQL_Query &q, d_Float f);
    friend d_OQL_Query &operator<<(d_OQL_Query &q, d_Double d);
    friend d_OQL_Query &operator<<(d_OQL_Query &q, const d_Date &d);
    friend d_OQL_Query &operator<<(d_OQL_Query &q, const d_Time &t);
    friend d_OQL_Query &operator<<(d_OQL_Query &q, const d_Timestamp &ts);
    friend d_OQL_Query &operator<<(d_OQL_Query &q, const d_Interval &i);
    template<class T> friend d_OQL_Query &operator<<(d_OQL_Query &q,
                                            const d_Ref<T> &r);
    template<class T> friend d_OQL_Query &operator<<(d_OQL_Query &q,
                                            const d_Collection<T> &q);
};
```

Strings used in the construction of a query may contain parameters signified by the form $i, where i is a number referring to the ith subsequent right operand in the construction of the query; the first subsequent right operand would be referred to as $1. If any of the $i are not followed by a right operand construction argument at the point d_oql_execute is called, a d_Error exception object of kind d_Error_QueryParameterCountInvalid is thrown. If the argument is of the wrong type, a d_Error exception object of kind d_Error_QueryParameterTypeInvalid is thrown.

Once a query has been executed via d_oql_execute, the arguments associated with the $i parameters are cleared and new arguments must be supplied. The original query string containing the $i parameters is retained across the call to d_oql_execute.

The d_OQL_Query copy constructor and assignment operator copy all the underlying data structures associated with the query, based upon the parameters that have been passed to the query at the point the operation is performed. If the original query object had two parameters passed to it, the object that is new or assigned to should have those same two parameters initialized. After either of these operations the two d_OQL_Query objects should be equivalent and have identical behavior.

Example:

Among the math students (computed before as in Section 5.4.1 into the variable mathematicians) who are teaching assistants and earn more than x, find the set of professors that they assist. Suppose there exists a named set of teaching assistants called "TA".

```
d_Set<d_Ref<Student> > mathematicians; // computed as above
d_Set<d_Ref<Professor> > assisted_profs;
double x = 50000.00;

d_OQL_Query q1 (
    "select t.assists.taught_by from t in TA where t.salary > $1 and t in $2");
q1 << x << mathematicians;
d_oql_execute( q1, assisted_profs);
```

After the above code has been executed, it could be followed by another query, passing in different arguments.

```
d_Set<d_Ref<Student> >historians;  // assume this gets computed similar
                                   // to mathematicians
double y = 40000.00

q1 << y << historians;
d_oql_execute( q1, assisted_profs);
```

The ODMG OQL implementation may have parsed, compiled, and optimized the original query; it can now re-execute the query with different arguments without incurring the overhead of compiling and optimizing the query.

5.5 Example

This section gives a complete example of a small C++ application. This application manages people records. A Person may be entered into the database. Then special events can be recorded: marriage, the birth of children, moving to a new address.

The application comprises two transactions: the first one populates the database, while the second consults and updates it.

The next section defines the schema of the database, as C++ ODL classes. The C++ program is given in the subsequent section.

5.5.1 Schema Definition

For the explanation of the semantics of this example, see Section 3.4, "Another Example." Here is the C++ ODL syntax:

```
// Schema Definition in C++ ODL
class City;              // forward declaration
struct Address {
    d_UShort        number;
    d_String        street;
    d_Ref<City>     city;
                    Address();
                    Address(d_UShort, const char*, const d_Ref<City> &);
};

extern const char _spouse [ ], _parents [ ], _children [ ] ;

class Person : public d_Object {
public:
// Attributes (all public, for this example)
    d_String                name;
    Address                 address;
// Relationships
    d_Rel_Ref<Person, _spouse>  spouse;
    d_Rel_List<Person, _parents> children;
    d_Rel_List<Person, _children> parents;
// Operations
                            Person(const char * pname);
    void                    birth(const d_Ref<Person> &child); // a child is born
    void                    marriage(const d_Ref<Person> &to_whom);
    d_Ref<d_Set<d_Ref<Person> > >ancestors() const; // returns ancestors
    void                    move(const Address &); // move to a new address
// Extent
static  d_Ref<d_Set<d_Ref<Person> > >    people; // a reference to class extent[1]
static  const char * const               extent_name;
```

---

1. This (transient) static variable will be initialized at transaction begin time (see the application).

```
};
class City : public d_Object {
public:
// Attributes
    d_ULong                          city_code;
    d_String                         name;
    d_Ref<d_Set<d_Ref<Person> > >   population;  // the people living in this City
// Operations
                                     City(int, const char*);
// Extension
static   d_Ref<d_Set<d_Ref<City> > >   cities;     // a reference to the class extent
static   const char * const            extent_name;
};
```

5.5.2 Schema Implementation

We now define the code of the operations declared in the schema. This is written in plain C++. We assume the C++ ODL preprocessor has generated a file, "schema.hxx", which contains the standard C++ definitions equivalent to the C++ ODL classes.

```
// Classes Implementation in C++
#include "schema.hxx"

const char _spouse [ ] = "spouse";
const char _parents [ ] = "parents";
const char _children [ ] = "children";

// Address structure:

Address::Address(d_UShort pnum, const char* pstreet,
                      const d_Ref<City> &pcity)
    : number(pnumber),
      street(pstreet),
      city(pcity)
{ }

Address::Address()
    : number(0),
      street(0),
      city(0)
{ }
// Person Class:
const char * const Person::extent_name = "people";
```

```
// Person Class:
const char * const Person::extent_name = "people";
Person::Person(const char * pname)
  :  name(pname)
{
     people->insert_element(this);  // Put this Person in the extension
}
void Person::birth(const d_Ref<Person> &child)
{                                          // Adds a new child to the children list
     children.insert_element_last(child);
     if(spouse)
          spouse->children.insert_element_last(child);
}
void Person::marriage(const d_Ref<Person> &to_whom)
{                                     // Initializes the spouse relationship
     spouse = with;                // with->spouse is automatically set to this Person
}
d_Ref<d_Set<d_Ref<Person> > >  Person::ancestors()
{                                     // Constructs the set of all ancestors of this Person
     d_Ref<d_Set<d_Ref<Person> > >  the_ancestors =
                                   new d_Set<d_Ref<Person> >;
     int i;
     for( i = 0; i < 2; i++)
          if( parents[i] ) {
               // The ancestors = parents union ancestors(parents)
               the_ancestors->insert_element(parents[i]);
               d_Ref<d_Set<d_Ref<Person> > >
grand_parents= parents[i]->ancestors();
               the_ancestors->union_with(*grand_parents);
               grand_parents.delete_object();
          }
     return the_ancestors;
}
void Person::move(const Address &new_address)
{                                          // Updates the address attribute of this Person
     if(address.city)
          address.city->population->remove_element(this);
     new_address.city->population->insert_element(this);
     mark_modified();[2]
     address = new_address;
}
```

```
// City class:

const char * const City::extent_name = "cities";

City::City(d_ULong code, const char * cname)
   :  city_code(code),
      name(cname)
{
      cities->insert_element(this);          // Put this City into the extension
}
```

5.5.3 An Application

We now have the whole schema well defined and implemented. We are able to populate the database and play with it. In the following application, the transaction Load builds some objects into the database. Then the transaction Consult reads it, prints some reports from it, and makes updates. Each transaction is implemented inside a C++ function.

The database is opened by the main program, which then starts the transactions.

```
#include <iostream.h>
#include "schema.hxx"

static d_Database dbobj;
static d_Database * database = &dbobj;

void Load()
{                            // Transaction which populates the database
      d_Transaction load;
      load.begin();
      // Create both Persons and Cities extensions, and name them.

      Person::people = new(database) d_Set<d_Ref<Person> >;
      City::cities = new(database) d_Set<d_Ref<City> >;

      database->set_object_name(Person::people, Person::extent_name);
      database->set_object_name(City::cities, City::extent_name);
```

---

2. Do not forget it! Notice that it is necessary only in the case where an attribute of the object is modified. When a relationship is updated, the object is automatically marked modified.

```
        // Construct 3 persistent objects from class Person.

        d_Ref<Person> God, Adam, Eve;

        God   = new(database, "Person") Person("God");
        Adam = new(database, "Person") Person("Adam");
        Eve   = new(database, "Person") Person("Eve");

    // Construct an Address structure, Paradise, as (7 Apple Street, Garden)
    // and set the address attributes of Adam and Eve.

        Address Paradise(7, "Apple", new(database, "City") City(0, "Garden"));

        Adam->move(Paradise);
        Eve->move(Paradise);

    // Define the family relationships.
        God->birth(Adam);
        Adam->marriage(Eve);
        Adam->birth(new(database, "Person") Person("Cain"));
        Adam->birth(new(database, "Person") Person("Abel"));

        load.commit();     // Commit transaction, putting objects into the database.
    }

    static void print_persons(const d_Collection<d_Ref<Person> >& s)
    {                               // A service function to print a collection of Persons
        d_Ref<Person> p;
        d_Iterator<d_Ref<Person> > it = s.create_iterator();
        while( it.next(p) ) {
            cout << "--- " << p->name << " lives in ";
            if (p->address.city)
                cout << p->address.city->name;
            else
                cout << "Unknown";
            cout << endl;
        }
    }
```

```
void Consult()
{                        // Transaction which consults and updates the database
    d_Transaction           consult;
    d_List<d_Ref<Person> >  list;
    consult.begin();
    // Static references to objects or collections must be recomputed
    // after a commit
    Person::people = database->lookup_object(Person::extent_name);
    City::cities = database->lookup_object(City::extent_name);
    // Now begin the transaction
    cout << "All the people ....:" << endl;
    print_persons(*Person::people);
    cout << "All the people sorted by name ....:" << endl;
    oql(list, "sort p in people by p.name");
    print_persons(list);
    cout << "People having 2 children and living in Paradise ...:" << endl;
    oql(list, " select p from p in people\
            where    p.address.city != nil and p.address.city.name = \"Garden\"\
                and count(p.children) = 2");
    print_persons(list);
    // Adam and Eve are moving ...
    Address Earth(13, "Macadam", new(database, "City") City(1, "St-Croix"));
    d_Ref<Person> Adam;
    oql( Adam, "element(select p from p in people where p.name = \"Adam\")" );
    Adam->move(Earth);
    Adam->spouse->move(Earth);
    cout << "Cain's ancestors ...:" << endl;
    d_Ref<Person> Cain = Adam->children.retrieve_element_at(0);
    print_persons(*(Cain->ancestors()));
    consult.commit();
}

main()
{
    database->open("family");
    Load();
    Consult();
    database->close();
}
```

Chapter 6

Smalltalk Binding

6.1 Introduction

This chapter defines the Smalltalk binding for the ODMG Object Model, ODL and OQL. While no Smalltalk language standard exists at this time, ODMG member organizations participate in the X3J20 ANSI Smalltalk standards committee. We expect that as standards are agreed upon by that committee and commercial implementations become available that the ODMG Smalltalk binding will evolve to accommodate them. In the interests of consistency and until an official Smalltalk standard exists, we will map many ODL concepts to class descriptions as specified by Smalltalk80.

6.1.1 Language Design Principles

The ODMG Smalltalk binding is based upon two principles: it should bind to Smalltalk in a natural way which is consistent with the principles of the language, and it should support language interoperability consistent with ODL specification and semantics. We believe that organizations who specify their objects in ODL will insist that the Smalltalk binding honor those specifications. These principles have several implications that are evident in the design of the binding described in the body of this chapter.

1. There is a unified type system which is shared by Smalltalk and the ODBMS. This type system is ODL as mapped into Smalltalk by the Smalltalk binding.

2. The binding respects the Smalltalk syntax, meaning the Smalltalk language will not have to be modified to accommodate this binding. ODL concepts will be represented using normal Smalltalk coding conventions.

3. The binding respects the fact that Smalltalk is dynamically typed. Arbitrary Smalltalk objects may be stored persistently, including ODL-specified objects which will obey the ODL typing semantics.

4. The binding respects the dynamic memory management semantics of Smalltalk. Objects will become persistent when they are referenced by other persistent objects in the database and will be removed when they are no longer reachable in this manner.

6.1.2 Language Binding

The ODMG binding for Smalltalk is based upon the recently adopted OMG Smalltalk IDL binding.[1] As ODL is a superset of IDL, the IDL binding defines a large part of the mapping required by this document. This chapter provides informal descriptions of the IDL binding topics and more formally defines the Smalltalk binding for the ODL extensions, including relationships, literals, and collections.

The ODMG Smalltalk binding can be generated by an ODL compiler which processes ODL declarations and generates a graph of *meta objects* which model the schema of the database. These meta objects would provide the type information which allows the Smalltalk binding to support the required ODL type semantics. The complete set of such meta objects would define the entire *schema* of the database and would serve much in the same capacity as an OMG Interface Repository.

In such a repository, the meta objects which represent the schema of the database would be programmatically accessed and modified by Smalltalk applications, through a standard interface. One such application, a *binding generator*, may be used to generate Smalltalk class and method skeletons from the meta objects. This binding generator would resolve the type/class mapping choices which are inherent in the ODMG Smalltalk binding.

The information in the meta objects is also sufficient to *regenerate* the ODL declarations for the portions of the schema which they represent. The relationships between these components are illustrated in Figure 6-1. A conforming implementation must support the Smalltalk output of this binding process; it need not provide automated tools.

In order to completely define the meta object interfaces which are needed to automate this binding process and fill the role of an ODBMS schema, further investigation is required. Such investigation must consider the relevant OMG Interface Repository standards, as well as the special needs of the ODBMS community. This is outside the scope of the current binding revision and will be considered for the next major release of the ODMG standard.

6.1.3 Mapping the ODMG Object Model into Smalltalk

Although Smalltalk provides a powerful data model that is close to the one presented in Chapter 2, it remains necessary to precisely describe how the concepts of the ODMG Object Model map into concrete Smalltalk constructions.

---

1. OMG Document 94-11-8, November 16, 1994

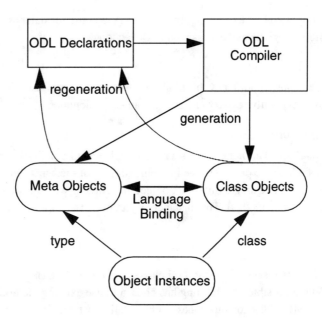

Figure 6-1. Smalltalk Language Binding

6.1.3.1 Object and Literal

An ODMG object type maps into a Smalltalk class. Since Smalltalk has no distinct notion of literal objects, both ODMG objects and ODMG literals may be implemented by the same Smalltalk classes.

6.1.3.2 Relationship

This concept is not directly supported by Smalltalk and must be implemented by Smalltalk methods which support a standard protocol. The relationship itself is typically implemented either as an object reference (one-to-one relation) or as an appropriate Collection subclass (one-to-many, many-to-many relations) embedded as an instance variable of the object. Rules for defining sets of accessor methods are presented which allow all relationships to be managed uniformly.

6.1.3.3 Names

Objects in Smalltalk have a unique object identity, and references to objects may appear in a variety of naming contexts. The Smalltalk system dictionary contains globally accessible objects which are indexed by Symbols which name them. A similar protocol has been defined on the Database class for managing named persistent objects which exist within the database. Other uses of Association and Dictionary classes may be managed by the programmer as needed.

6.1.3.4 Extents

Extents are not supported by this binding. Instead, users may use the database naming protocol to explicitly register and access named Collections.

6.1.3.5 Keys

Key declarations are not supported by this binding. Instead, users may use the database naming protocol to explicitly register and access named Dictionaries.

6.1.3.6 Implementation

Everything in Smalltalk is implemented as an object. Objects in Smalltalk have instance variables which are private to the implementations of their methods. An instance variable refers to a single Smalltalk object, the class of which is available at runtime through the class method. This instance object may itself refer to other objects.

6.1.3.7 Collections

Smalltalk provides a rich set of Collection subclasses, including Set, Bag, List, and Array classes. Where possible, this binding has chosen to use existing methods to implement the ODMG Collection interfaces. Unlike statically typed languages, Smalltalk collections may contain heterogeneous elements whose type is only known at runtime.   Implementations utilizing these collections must be able to enforce the homogeneous type constraints of ODL.

6.1.3.8 Database Administration

Databases are represented by instances of Database objects in this binding, and a protocol is defined for creating databases and for connecting to them. Some operations regarding database administration are not addressed by this binding and represent opportunities for future work.

6.2 Smalltalk ODL Binding

6.2.1 OMG IDL Binding Overview

Since the Smalltalk/ODL binding is based upon the OMG Smalltalk/IDL binding, we include here some descriptions of the important aspects of the IDL binding which are needed in order to better understand the ODL binding which follows. These descriptions are not intended to be definitions of these aspects, however, and the reader should consult the OMG binding document directly for the actual definitions.

6.2.1.1 Identifiers

IDL allows the use of underscore characters in its identifiers. Since underscore characters are not allowed in all Smalltalk implementations, the Smalltalk/IDL binding provides a conversion algorithm. To convert an IDL identifier with underscores into a Smalltalk identifier, remove the underscore and capitalize the following letter (if it exists).

6.2.1.2 Interfaces

Interfaces define sets of operations which an instance which supports that interface must possess. As such, interfaces correspond to Smalltalk protocols. Implementors are free to map interfaces to classes as required to specify the operations which are supported by a Smalltalk object. In the IDL binding, all objects which have an IDL definition must implement a CORBAName method which returns the fully scoped name of an interface which defines all of its IDL behavior.

> anObject CORBAName

6.2.1.3 Objects

Any Smalltalk object which has an associated IDL definition (by its CORBAName method) may be a CORBA object. In addition, many Smalltalk objects may also represent instances of IDL types as defined below.

6.2.1.4 Operations

IDL operations allow zero or more *in* parameters and may also return a functional result. Unlike Smalltalk, IDL operations also allow *out* and *inout* parameters to be defined which allow more than a single result to be communicated back to the caller of the method. In the Smalltalk/IDL binding, holders for these return parameters are passed explicitly by the caller in the form of objects which support the CORBAParameter protocol (value, value:). IDL operation signatures also differ in syntax from that of Smalltalk selectors, and the IDL binding specifies a mapping rule for composing default selectors from the operation and parameter names of the IDL definition. The binding allows default selectors to be explicitly overridden, allowing flexibility in method naming.

6.2.1.5 Types

Since, in Smalltalk, everything is an object, there is no separation of objects and datatypes as exist in other hybrid languages such as C++. Thus it is necessary for some Smalltalk objects to fill dual roles in the binding. Since some objects in Smalltalk are more natural in this role than others, we will describe the simple type mappings first.

Simple Types

IDL allows several basic datatypes which are similar to literal valued objects in Smalltalk. While exact type-class mappings are not specified in the IDL binding for technical reasons, the following mappings comply:

- short, unsigned short, long, unsigned long — An appropriate Integer object
- float, double — An appropriate LimitedPrecisionReal object

- char — An appropriate Character object
- boolean — The values **true** and **false**
- octet — An appropriate Integer object to represent [0 .. 255] values
- string — An appropriate String object
- any — Any Smalltalk object which supports CORBAName

Complicated Types

IDL has a number of data structuring mechanisms which have a less intuitive mapping to Smalltalk. The list below describes the *implicit* bindings for these types. Implementors are also free to provide *explicit* bindings for these types which allow other Smalltalk objects to be used in these roles. These explicit bindings are especially important in the ODL binding since the various Collections have an object-literal duality which is not present in IDL (e.g., ODL list sequences also have a List interface).

- Array — An appropriate Array instance
- Sequence — An appropriate OrderedCollection instance
- Structure — A Dictionary containing the fields of the structure
- Union — Implicit: Any Smalltalk object with a CORBAName
- Union — Explicit: A Smalltalk object which supports the CORBAUnion protocol (discriminator, discriminator:, value, and value: methods)
- Enum — Smalltalk objects which support the CORBAEnum protocol (=, <, > methods)

6.2.1.6 Exceptions

IDL Exceptions are defined within modules and interfaces, and are referenced by the operation signatures which raise them. Each exception may define a set of alternative results which are returned to the caller should the exception be raised by the operation. These values are similar to structures, and Dictionaries are used to represent exception values.

6.2.1.7 Constants

Constants, Exceptions, and Enums which are defined in IDL are made available to the Smalltalk programmer in a global dictionary CORBAConstants, which is indexed by the fully qualified scoped name of the IDL entity.

6.2.2 Smalltalk ODL Binding Extensions

This section describes the binding of ODMG ODL to Smalltalk. ODL provides a description of the database schema as a set of interfaces, including their attributes, relationships, and operations. Smalltalk implementations consist of a set of object classes and their instances. The language binding provides a mapping between these domains.

6.2.2.1 Interfaces

In IDL, interfaces are used to represent the *abstract behavior* of an object which is visible to clients in a distributed systems environment. ODL interfaces, while syntactically equivalent in most ways, are additionally used to model the *abstract state* of objects in an ODBMS. This application is inherently more concrete and closer to the implementation level than the IDL mission. In a distributed system using ODBMS object persistence, the ODL interfaces which define the object's abstract state could be expected to inherit from IDL interfaces which define the portions of the object's behavior which is visible to remote clients. The exact roles of IDL and ODL interfaces in such a hybrid system is a topic for future versions of this binding.

In order to maintain the separation of ODMG ODL and OMG IDL interpretations of interface definitions, all uses of the method CORBAName in the IDL binding will be replaced by the method ODLName in this definition. This method will return the name of the ODL interface which is bound to the object.

    aDate ODLName

returns the string '::Date' which is the name of its ODL interface. Similarly, all uses of the CORBAConstants dictionary for constants, enums, and exceptions will be replaced by a global dictionary named ODLConstants in this definition. For example:

    (ODLConstants at: #'::Date::Monday')

is a Weekday enum,

    (ODLConstants at: #'::Time::USPacific')

equals -8, and

    (ODLConstants at: #'::Iterator::NoMoreElements')

is an Exception.

6.2.2.2 Attribute Declarations

Attribute declarations are used to define pairs of accessor operations which *get* and *set* attribute values. Generally, there will be a one-to-one correspondence between attributes defined within an interface and instance variables defined within a class, although this is not required. Syntactically, ODL attribute declarations are identical to those of IDL. Semantically, however, ODL attributes define the *abstract state* of their object, whereas in IDL they are merely a convenience mechanism for introducing get and set accessing operations.

For example:

    attribute Enum Rank {full, associate, assistant} rank;

yields Smalltalk methods:

    rank
    rank: aProfessorRank

6.2.2.3 Relationship Declarations

Relationships define sets of accessor operations for adding and removing associations between objects. As with attributes, relationships are a part of an object's *abstract state*. The Smalltalk binding for relationships results in public methods to *form* and *drop* members from the relationship, plus public methods on the relationship target classes to provide access and private methods to manage the required referential integrity constraints. We begin the relationship binding by introducing a mapping rule from ODL relationships to equivalent IDL constructions, and then illustrate with a complete example.

Single-valued Relationships

For single-value relationships such as

```
relationship  X  Y              inverse  Z;
```

we expand first to the IDL attribute and operations:

```
attribute       X   Y;
void            form_Y(in X target);
void            drop_Y(in X target);
```

which results in the following Smalltalk selectors:

```
Y
formY:
dropY:
Y:                                "private"
```

For example, from Chapter 2:

```
interface Course {
...
    relationship Professor is_taught_by
        inverse Professor::teaches;
...
}
```

yields Smalltalk methods (on the class Course):

```
formIsTaughtBy: aProfessor
dropIsTaughtBy: aProfessor
isTaughtBy
isTaughtBy:                       "private"
```

Multi-valued Relationships

For a multi-valued ODL relationship such as

```
relationship   set<X>           Y inverse Z;
```

we expand first to the IDL attribute and operations:

```
readonly attribute              set<X>          Y;
void            form_Y(in X target);
void            drop_Y(in X target);
void            add_Y(in X target);
void            remove_Y(in X target);
```

which results in the following Smalltalk selectors:

```
Y
formY:
dropY:
addY:          "private"
removeY:       "private"
```

For example, from Chapter 2:

```
interface Professor {

...
    relationship Set<Course> teaches
        inverse Course::is_taught_by;
...
}
```

yields Smalltalk methods (on class Professor):

```
formTeaches: aCourse
dropTeaches: aCourse
teaches

addTeaches: aCourse          "private"
removeTeaches: aCourse       "private"
```

Finally, to form the above relationship, the programmer could write

```
| professor course |

professor := Professor new.
course := Course new.
professor formTeaches: course.
    -or-
course formIsTaughtBy: professor.
```

6.2.2.4 Collections

Chapter 2 introduced several new kinds of Collections which extend the IDL sequence to deal with the special needs of ODBMS users. The following table shows the Smalltalk method selector which this binding defines for each of the Collection interfaces. Where possible, we have explicitly bound operations to commonly available

Smalltalk80 selectors when the default operation binding rules would not produce the desired selector. These are indicated in the table as *explicit* bindings.

TABLE 6-1. Smalltalk Operation Protocols for ODL Collections

Collection Operations	Selector	Binding
::Collection::cardinality	size	explicit
::Collection::is_empty	isEmpty	default
::Collection::insert_element	add:	explicit
::Collection::remove_element	remove:	explicit
::Collection::contains_element	includes:	explicit
::Collection::create_iterator	createIterator	default

Bag Operations	Selector	Binding
::Bag::union_with	union:	explicit
::Bag::intersection_with	intersection:	explicit
::Bag::difference_with	difference:	explicit

Set Operations	Selector	Binding
::Set::union_with	union:	explicit
::Set::intersection_with	intersection:	explicit
::Set::difference_with	difference:	explicit
::Set::is_subset_of	isSubset:	explicit
::Set::is_proper_subset_of	isProperSubset:	explicit
::Set::is_superset_of	isSuperset:	explicit
::Set::is_proper_superset_of	isProperSuperset:	explicit

List Operations	Selector	Binding
::List::replace_element_at	at:put:	explicit
::List::remove_element_at	removeAtIndex:	explicit
::List::retrieve_element_at	at:	explicit
::List::insert_element_after	add:after:	explicit
::List::insert_element_before	add:before:	explicit
::List::insert_element_first	addFirst:	explicit
::List::insert_element_last	addLast:	explicit
::List::remove_first_element	removeFirst	explicit
::List::remove_last_element	removeLast	explicit
::List::retrieve_first_element	first	explicit

TABLE 6-1. Smalltalk Operation Protocols for ODL Collections *(Continued)*

::List::retrieve_last_element	last	explicit
::List::concat	,	explicit
::List::append	addAll:	explicit

Array Operations	**Selector**	**Binding**
::Array::replace_element_at	at:put:	explicit
::Array::remove_element_at	removeElementAt:	default
::Array::retrieve_element_at	at:	explicit
::Array::resize	changeSizeTo:	explicit

Iterator Operations	**Selector**	**Binding**
::Iterator::not_done	notDone	default
::Iterator::next	nextElement:	explicit
::Iterator::advance	next	explicit
::Iterator::get_element	peek	explicit
::Iterator::reset	reset	default

6.2.2.5 Structured Literals

Chapter 2 defined structured literals to represent Date, Time, Timestamp, and Interval values which must be supported by each language binding. The following table defines the binding from each operation to the appropriate Smalltalk selector and indicates whether the binding is default or explicit.

TABLE 6-2. Smalltalk Operation Protocols for ODL Literals

Date Operations	**Selector**	**Binding**
::Date::year	year	default
::Date::month	month	default
::Date::day	day	default
::Date::day_of_year	dayOfYear	default
::Date::month_of_year	monthOfYear	default
::Date::day_of_week	dayOfWeek	default
::Date::is_leap_year	isLeapYear	default
::Date::is_equal	=	explicit

TABLE 6-2. Smalltalk Operation Protocols for ODL Literals *(Continued)*

::Date::is_greater	>	explicit
::Date::is_greater_or_equal	>=	explicit
::Date::is_less	<	explicit
::Date::is_less_or_equal	<=	explicit
::Date::is_between	isBetween:and:	explicit
::Date::next	next:	default
::Date::previous	previous:	default
::Date::add_days	addDays:	default
::Date::subtract_days	subtractDays:	default
::Date::subtract_date	subtractDate:	default

Interval Operations	**Selector**	**Binding**
::Interval::day	day	default
::Interval::hour	hour	default
::Interval::minute	minute	default
::Interval::second	second	default
::Interval::is_zero	isZero	default
::Interval::plus	plus:	default
::Interval::minus	minus:	default
::Interval::product	product:	default
::Interval::quotient	quotient:	default
::Interval::is_equal	=	explicit
::Interval::is_greater	>	explicit
::Interval::is_greater_or_equal	>=	explicit
::Interval::is_less	<	explicit
::Interval::is_less_or_equal	<=	explicit

Time Operations	**Selector**	**Binding**
::Time::hour	hour	default
::Time::minute	minute	default
::Time::second	second	default
::Time::tz_hour	tzHour	default
::Time::tz_minute	tzMinute	default

TABLE 6-2. Smalltalk Operation Protocols for ODL Literals *(Continued)*

::Time::is_equal	=	explicit
::Time::is_greater	>	explicit
::Time::is_greater_or_equal	>=	explicit
::Time::is_less	<	explicit
::Time::is_less_or_equal	<=	explicit
::Time::is_between	isBetween:and:	explicit
::Time::add_interval	addInterval:	default
::Time::subtract_interval	subtractInterval:	default
::Time::subtract_time	subtractTime:	default
TimeStamp Operations	**Selector**	**Binding**
::TimeStamp::the_date	asDate	explicit
::TimeStamp::the_time	asTime	explicit
::TimeStamp::year	year	default
::TimeStamp::month	month	default
::TimeStamp::day	day	default
::TimeStamp::hour	hour	default
::TimeStamp::minute	minute	default
::TimeStamp::second	second	default
::TimeStamp::tz_hour	tzHour	default
::TimeStamp::tz_minute	tzMinute	default
::TimeStamp::plus	+	explicit
::TimeStamp::minus	-	explicit
::TimeStamp::is_equal	=	explicit
::TimeStamp::is_greater	>	explicit
::TimeStamp::is_greater_or_equal	>=	explicit
::TimeStamp::is_less	<	explicit
::TimeStamp::is_less_or_equal	<=	explicit
::TimeStamp::is_between	isBetween:and:	explicit

6.2.2.6 Factory Interfaces

Chapter 2 introduced interfaces which define the operations on several Collection and Literal objects. These interfaces define the instance protocols but do not define the

associated class protocols for these objects. In the following, we introduce ODL definitions of *Factory interfaces* for these class objects and then provide a similar binding
table.

```
interface ObjectFactory {
    Object          create();
};


interface CollectionFactory {
    Collection      create(in unsigned long size);
};


interface DateFactory {
    exception       InvalidDate{};

    typedef         unsigned short                      ushort;

    Date            julian_date(in ushort, in ushort julian_day);
    Date            calendar_date(in ushort year,
                                  in ushort month,
                                  in ushort day)    raises(InvalidDate);

    boolean         is_leap_year(in ushort year);
    boolean         is_valid(in ushort year,
                             in ushort month,
                             in ushort day);

    ushort          days_in_year(in ushort year);
    ushort          days_in_month(in ushort year, in Date::Month mo);
    Date            today();
};


interface TimeFactory {
    typedef         unsigned short                      ushort;

    attribute       Time::Time_Zone                     default_time_zone;
    Time            from_hms(in ushort hour,
                             in ushort minute,
                             in float second);
    Time            from_hmstz(in ushort hour,
                               in ushort minute,
                               in float second,
                               in short tz_hour,
                               in short tz_minute);
    Time            current();
};


interface TimeStampFactory {
    TimeStamp   current();
    TimeStamp   create(in Date a_date, in Time a_time);
};
```

TABLE 6-3. Smalltalk Operation Protocols for Factory Interfaces

ObjectFactory Operations	Selector	Binding
::ObjectFactory::create	new	explicit

CollectionFactory Operations	Selector	Binding
::CollectionFactory::create	new:	explicit

DateFactory Operations	Selector	Binding
::DateFactory::julian_date	julianDate:julianDay:	default
::DateFactory::calendar_date	calendarDate:month:day:	default
::DateFactory::is_leap_year	isLeapYear:	default
::DateFactory::is_valid	isValid:month:day:	default
::DateFactory::days_in_year	daysInYear:	default
::DateFactory::days_in_month	daysInMonth:mo:	default
::DateFactory::current	today	explicit

TimeFactory Operations	Selector	Binding
::TimeFactory::from_hms	fromHms:-minute:second:	default
::TimeFactory::from_hmstz	fromHmstz:-minute:second:-tzHour:tzMinute:	default
::TimeFactory::current	current	default

TimeStampFactory Operations	Selector	Binding
::TimeStampFactory::current	now	explicit
::TimeStampFactory::create	fromDate:andTime:	explicit

6.3 Smalltalk OML

The Smalltalk Object Manipulation Language (OML) consists of a set of method additions to the classes Object and Behavior, plus the classes Database and Transaction. The guiding principle in the design of Smalltalk OML is that the syntax used to create, delete, identify, reference, get/set property values, and invoke operations on a persistent object should be no different from that used for objects of shorter lifetimes. A single expression may thus freely intermix references to persistent and transient objects. All Smalltalk OML operations are invoked by sending messages to appropriate objects.

6.3.1 Object Protocol

Since all Smalltalk objects inherit from class Object, it is natural to implement some of the ODMG language binding mechanisms as methods on this class.

6.3.1.1 Object Persistence

Persistence is not limited to any particular subset of the class hierarchy, nor is it determined at object creation time. A transient object that participates in a relationship with a persistent object will become persistent when a transaction commit occurs. This approach is called *transitive persistence*.

6.3.1.2 Object Deletion

In the Smalltalk binding, as in Smalltalk, there is no notion of explicit deletion of objects. An object is removed from the database during garbage collection if that object is not referenced by any other persistent object.

6.3.1.3 Object Locking

Objects activated into memory acquire the default lock for the active concurrency control policy. Optionally, a lock can be explicitly acquired on an object by sending the appropriate locking message to it. Two locking mode enumeration values are required to be supported: read and write. The OMG Concurrency service's LockSet interface is the source of the following method definitions.

To acquire a lock on an object which will block the process until success, the syntax would be

        anObject lock: aLockMode.

To acquire a lock without blocking, the syntax would be

        anObject tryLock: aLockMode. "returns a boolean indicating
                        success or failure"

In these methods, the receiver is locked in the context of the current transaction. A lockNotGrantedSignal is raised by the lock: method if the requested lock cannot be granted. Locks are released implicitly at the end of the transaction, unless an option to retain locks is used.

6.3.1.4 Object Modification

Modified persistent Smalltalk objects will have their updated values reflected in the ODBMS at transaction commit. Persistent objects to be modified must be sent the message markModified. MarkModified prepares the receiver object by setting a write lock (if it does not already have a write lock) and marking it so that the ODBMS can detect that the object has been modified.

    anObject markModified

It is conventional to send the markModified message as part of each method that sets an instance variable's value. Immutable objects, such as instances of Character and SmallInteger and instances such as **nil**, **true**, and **false**, cannot change their intrinsic values. The markModified message has no effect on these objects. Sending markModified to a transient object is also a null operation.

6.3.2 Database Protocol

An object called a Database is used to manage each connection with a database. A Smalltalk application must open a Database before any objects in that database are accessible. A Database object may only be connected to a single database at a time; however, a vendor may allow many concurrent Databases to be open on different databases simultaneously.

6.3.2.1 Opening a Database

To open a new database, send the open: method to an instance of the Database class.

```
database := Database new.
... set additional parameters as required ...
database open: aDatabaseName
```

If the connection is not established, a connectionFailedSignal will be raised.

6.3.2.2 Closing a Database

To close a database, send the close message to the Database.

    aDatabase close

This closes the connection to the particular database. Once the connection is closed, further attempts to access the database will raise a notConnectedSignal. A Database which has been closed may be subsequently reopened using the open method defined above.

6.3.2.3 Database Names

Each Database manages a persistent name space which maps symbols to objects or collections of objects which are contained in the database. The following paragraphs describe the methods which are used to manage this name space. In addition to being assigned an object identifier by the ODBMS, an individual object may be given a name that is meaningful to the programmer or end-user. Each database provides methods for associating names with objects and for determining the names of given objects. Named objects become the roots from which the Smalltalk binding's transitive persistence policy is computed.

The bind:name: method is used to name any persistent object in a database.

aDatabase bind: anObject name: aSymbol

The lookup:ifAbsent: method is used to retrieve the object which is associated with the given name. If no such object exists in the database, the absentBlock will be evaluated.

aDatabase lookup: aNameSymbol ifAbsent: absentBlock

6.3.3 Transaction Protocol

6.3.3.1 Global Transactions

Transactions are implemented in Smalltalk using methods defined on the class Transaction. Transactions are dynamically scoped, and may be started, committed, aborted, and checkpointed. The default concurrency policy is pessimistic concurrency control (see Locking, above), but an ODBMS may support additional policies as well. With the pessimistic policy all access, creation, modification, and deletion of persistent objects must be done within a transaction.

A transaction may be started by invoking the method begin on the Transaction class.

Transaction begin

A transaction is committed by sending the message commit to Transaction. This causes the transaction to commit, writing the changes to all persistent objects which have been modified within the context of the transaction to the database.

Transaction commit

Transient objects are not subject to transaction semantics. Committing a transaction does not remove transient objects from memory, nor does aborting a transaction restore the state of modified transient objects. The method for executing block-scoped transactions (below) provides a mechanism to deal with transient objects.

A transaction may also be checkpointed by sending the checkpoint message to Transaction. This is equivalent to performing a commit followed by a begin, except that all locks are retained and the transaction's identity is preserved.

Transaction checkpoint

Checkpointing can be useful in order to continue working with the same objects while ensuring that intermediate logical results are written to the database.

A transaction may be aborted by sending the abort message to Transaction. This causes the transaction to end and all changes to persistent objects made within the context of that transaction will be rolled back in the database.

Transaction abort

6.3.3.2 Block-Scoped Transactions

A transaction can also be scoped to a Block to allow for greater convenience and integrity. The following method on class Transaction evaluates aBlock within the context of a new transaction. If the transaction commits, the commitBlock will be evaluated after the commit has completed. If the transaction aborts, the abortBlock will be evaluated after the rollback has completed. The abortBlock may be used to undo any side effects of the transaction on transient objects.

```
Transaction perform: aBlock
    onAbort: abortBlock
    onCommit: commitBlock
```

Within the transaction block, the checkpoint message may be used without terminating the transaction.

6.3.3.3 Transaction Exceptions

Several exceptions which may be raised during the execution of a transaction are defined:

- The noTransactionSignal is raised if an attempt is made to access persistent objects outside of a valid transaction context.
- The inactiveSignal is raised if a transactional operation is attempted in the context of a transaction which has already committed or aborted.
- The transactionCommitFailedSignal is raised if a commit operation is unsuccessful.

6.4 Smalltalk OQL

Chapter 4 defined the Object Query Language. This section describes how OQL is mapped to the Smalltalk language. The current Smalltalk OQL binding is a loosely coupled binding modeled after the OMG Object Query Service Specification. A future binding may include one which is more tightly integrated with the Smalltalk language.

6.4.1 Query Class

Instances of the class Query have four attributes: queryResult, queryStatus, queryString, and queryParameters. The queryResult holds the object that was the result of executing the OQL query. The queryStatus holds the status of query execution. The queryString is the OQL query text to be executed. The queryParameters contains variable/value pairs to be bound to the OQL query at execution.

The Query class supports the following methods:

```
create: aQueryString params: aParameterList      "returns a Query"
evaluate: aQueryString params: aParameterList    "returns query result"
complete                                         "returns enum complete"
incomplete                                       "returns enum incomplete"
```

Instances of the Query class support the following methods:

```
prepare: aParameterList     "no result"
execute: aParameterList     "no result"
getResult                   "returns the query result"
getStatus                   "returns a QueryStatus"
```

The execute: and prepare: methods can raise the QueryProcessingError signal if an error in the query is detected. The queryString may include parameters specified by the form $variable, where variable is a valid Smalltalk Integer. Parameter lists may be partially specified by Dictionaries and fully specified by Arrays or OrderedCollections.

Example:

Return all persons older than 45 who weigh less than 150. Assume there exists a collection of People called AllPeople.

```
| query result |
query := Query
    create: 'select name from AllPeople where age > $1 and weight < $2'
    params: #(45 150).
query execute: Dictionary new.
[query getStatus = Query complete] whileFalse: [Processor yield].
result := query getResult.
```

To return all persons older than 45 that weigh less than 170, the same Query instance could be reused. This would save the overhead of parsing and optimizing the query again.

```
query execute: (Dictionary with: 2->170).
[query getStatus = Query complete] whileFalse: [Processor yield].
result := query getResult.
```

The following example illustrates the simple, synchronous form of querying an OQL database. This query will return the bag of the names of customers from the same state as aCustomer.

```
Query
    evaluate: 'select c.name from AllCustomers c where c.address.state = $1'
    params: (Array with: aCustomer address state)
```

6.5 Future Directions

A number of important aspects of Smalltalk access to ODBMS databases remain to be standardized in order to increase portability and interoperability in application deployment. These topics have been touched upon in the preceding sections, but more work remains to formalize them enough to be in this standard.

A set of standard Meta Object interfaces would enable the development of tools for designing, building, and administering ODBMS interface repository schemas and would allow the binding processes to be more fully automated. These interfaces need to account for the particular needs of ODBMSs and need to be positioned with respect to the relevant OMG standards for IDL Interface Repositories.

Many people believe that keys and extents are an essential ingredient of database query processing. Implicit extents and keys would be preferable to explicit mechanisms involving named Collections, yet there are challenging engineering issues which must be faced to rationalize these capabilities with the notions of transitive persistence and dynamic storage management herein presented.

A uniform set of Database administration operations would facilitate application portability and allow system administration tools to be constructed which could work uniformly across multiple vendors' database products.

This binding has only touched upon the need for interface regeneration mechanisms. Such mechanisms would allow programmers with existing applications utilizing language-specific and even database-specific ODL mechanisms to produce the interface definitions which would insulate them from the differences between these mechanisms.

Object databases using ODL for their schema definitions can be effective as persistence mechanisms for Object Request Brokers in heterogeneous distributed systems. We need to better understand and define the exact roles of IDL and ODL interfaces in these systems. The need for distributed transactions in such systems is critical in order to guarantee proper operation of distributed applications in enterprise computing environments. Finally, full support for nested transactions in these systems can also allow for increased levels of uniformity and modularity of failure recovery.

Appendix A

Comparison with OMG Object Model

A.1 Introduction

This appendix compares the ODMG Object Model outlined in Chapter 2 of this specification with the OMG Object Model as outlined in Chapter 4 of the *OMG Architecture Guide*.

The bottom line is that the ODMG Object Model (ODMG/OM) is a superset of the OMG Object Model (OMG/OM).

The subsections of this appendix discuss the purpose of the two models and how the ODMG/OM fits into the component/profile structure defined by the OMG/OM, and review the capability between the two models in the major areas defined by the OMG/OM: types, instances, objects, and operations.

A.2 Purpose

The OMG/OM states that its primary objective is to support application portability. Three levels of portability are called out: (1) design portability, (2) source code portability, and (3) object code portability. The OMG/OM focused on design portability. The ODMG/OM goes a step further — to source code portability. The OMG/OM distinguishes two other dimensions of portability: portability across technology domains (e.g., a common object model across GUI, PL, and DBMS domains), and portability across products from different vendors within a technology domain (e.g., across ODBMS products from different vendors). The ODMG/OM focuses on portability within the technology domain of object database management systems. The ODMG standards suite is designed to allow application builders to write to a single ODBMS application programming interface (API), in the assurance that this API will be supported by a wide range of ODBMS vendors. The ODMG/OM defines the semantics of the object types that make up this API. Subsequent chapters within the ODMG standard define the syntactic forms through which this model is bound to specific programming languages.

To offer real portability, a standard has to support a level of DBMS functionality rich enough to meet the needs of the applications expected to use the standard. It cannot define such a low-level API that real applications need to use functionality supplied only by vendor-specific extensions to the API. The low-level, least-common-denominator approach taken in the standards for relational data management has meant that real applications need to use functionality supplied only by vendor-specific extensions to the API. Several studies in the late 1980s that analyzed large bodies of applications written against the relational API (SQL) showed that 30–40% of the RDBMS calls in the application are actually "standard SQL"; the other 60–70% use vendor-specific extensions. The result is that the relational standard does not in practice deliver the source-code-level application portability that it promised. The ODMG APIs have been designed to provide a much higher level of functionality and therefore a much higher degree of application portability.

A.3 Components and Profiles

The OMG Object Model is broken into a set of *components,* with a distinguished "Core Component" that defines objects and operations. The theory espoused by the OMG is that each "technology domain" (GUI, ODBMS, etc.) will assemble a set of these components into a *profile.* Figure A-1 illustrates this. Two profiles are shown — the Object Request Broker (ORB) profile and the Object DBMS (ODBMS) profile.

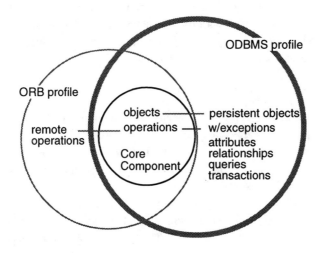

Figure A-1

The ORB profile includes the Core Component plus support for remote operations. The ODBMS profile includes the Core Component plus support for

- persistent objects
- properties (attributes and relationships)
- queries
- transactions

It also strengthens the core component definition of operations by including exception returns.

To date, the only OMG/OM component that has been defined is the Core Component. The additional functionality included in the ORB profile has not been formally specified as a set of named components. Nor are there OMG component definitions for the functionality expected to be added by the ODBMS profile. One of the reasons for making the comparison between the OMG/OM (i.e., the Core Component) is that the members of ODMG expect to submit definitions of each of the items in the bulleted list above as candidate *components*, and the sum of them as a candidate *profile* for object database management systems. Since the submitting companies collectively represent 80+% of the commercially available ODBMS products on the market, we assume that adoption of an ODBMS profile along the lines of that outlined in Chapter 2 will move through the OMG process relatively quickly.

The OMG/OM is outlined below, with indications how the ODMG/OM agrees.

Types, Instances, Interfaces, and Implementations:
- Objects are instances of types.
- A type defines the behavior and state of its instances.
- Behavior is specified as a set of operations.
- An object can be an immediate instance of only one type.
- The type of an object is determined statically at the time the object is created; objects do not dynamically acquire and lose types.
- Types are organized into a subtype/supertype graph.
- A type may have multiple supertypes.
- Supertypes are explicitly specified; subtype/supertype relationships between types are not deduced from signature compatibility of the types.

Operations:
- Operations have signatures that specify the operation name, arguments, and return values.
- Operations are defined on a single type — the type of their distinguished first argument — rather than on two types.
- Operations may take either literals or objects as their arguments. Semantics of argument passing is pass by reference.
- Operations are invoked.
- Operations may have side effects.
- Operations are implemented by methods in the implementation portion of the type definition.

The OMG/OM does not currently define exception returns on operations; it says that it expects there to be an exception-handling component defined outside of the core model. The ODMG/OM does define exception returns to operations.

A.4 Type Hierarchy

The fact that the ODMG/OM is a superset of the OMG/OM can also be seen by looking at the built-in type hierarchy defined by the two models. Figure A-2 shows the ODMG/OM type hierarchy. The types whose names are shown in italics are those which are also defined in the OMG/OM. As in Chapter 2, indenting is used to show subtype/supertype relationships, e.g., the type Collection is a subtype of the type Object-type.

- *Literal_type*
  - *Atomic_literal*
  - *Collection_literal*
  - *Structured_literal*
- *Object_type*
  - *Atomic_object*
  - *Collection*

Figure A-2

The ODMG/OM is a richer model than the OMG/OM — particularly in its support for properties and in its more detailed development of a subtype hierarchy below the types Object and Literal. The only differences between the two models in the areas common to them are two type names. The type that is called Literal in the ODMG/OM is called Non-Object in the OMG/OM. Although the OMG/OM does not formally introduce a supertype of the types Object and Non-Object, in the body of the document it refers to instances of these two types as the set of all "denotable values" or "Dvals" in the model. In the ODMG/OM a common supertype for Object and Literal is defined. The instances of type Object are mutable; they are therefore given OIDs in the ODMG/OM; although the value of the object may change, its OID is invariant. The OID can therefore be used to denote the object. Literals, by contrast, are immutable. Since the instances of a literal type are distinguished from one another by their value, this value can be used directly to denote the instance. There is no need to ascribe separate OIDs to literals.

In summary, the ODMG/OM is a clean superset of the OMG/OM.

A.5 The ORB profile

A second question could be raised. One product category has already been approved by the OMG — the ORB. To what extent are the non-core components implicit in that product consistent or inconsistent with their counterpart non-core components in the ODMG/OM? There is some divergence in literals, inheritance semantics, and operations — the latter because the ORB restricts in two key ways the semantics already defined in the OMG core object model: object identity and the semantics of arguments passed to operations. Those battles, however, are not ours. They are between the

OMG ORB task force and the OMG Object Model task force. The requirement placed on a prospective ODBMS task force is simply that the set of components included in the ODBMS profile include the Core Component — objects and operations. This appendix addresses that question.

A.6 Other Standards Groups

There are several standards organizations in the process of defining object models.

1. Application-specific standards groups that have defined an object model as a basis for their work in defining schemas of common types in their application domain, e.g.,

   - CFI (electrical CAD)
   - PDES/STEP (mechanical CAD)
   - ODA (computer-aided publishing)
   - PCTE (CASE)
   - OSI/NMF (telephony)
   - ANSI X3H6 (CASE)
   - ANSI X3H4 (IRDS reference model)

2. Formal standards bodies working on generic object models, e.g.,

   - ISO ODP
   - ANSI X3H7 (Object Information Systems)
   - ANSI X3T5.4 (managed objects)
   - ANSI X3T3

It is our current working assumption that the OMG-promulgated interface definitions for ORB and ODBMS will have sufficiently broad support across software vendors and hardware manufacturers that interface definitions put in the public domain through the OMG and supported by commercial vendors will develop the kind of de facto market share that has historically been an important prerequisite to adoption by ANSI and ISO. Should that prove not to be the case, the ODMG will make direct proposals to ANSI and ISO once the member companies of ODMG and their customers have developed a base of experience with the proposed API through use of commercial ODBMS products that support this API.

Appendix B

ODBMS in the OMG ORB Environment

B.1 Introduction

The existing documents of OMG do not yet address the issue of how an ODBMS fits into the OMG environment and, in particular, how it communicates with and cooperates with the ORB. This fundamental architectural issue is critical to the success of users of the OMG environment who also need ODBMSs.

This document is a position statement of the ODMG defining the desired architecture. It explicitly does not discuss the architecture of the internals of an ODBMS implementation but rather leaves that to the implementor of the ODBMS. Instead, it discusses how the ODBMS fits architecturally into the larger OMG environment.

The issues for a successful fit are the following:

- performance — e.g., direct object access
- distribution and heterogeneity — as managed by ODBMS for fine-grained objects
- ODBMS as Object Manager — responsible for multiple objects
- common repository — ability of ORB to use ODBMS as repository
- ODBMS as a user of the ORB — ability of ODBMS to use the services provided by the ORB (including other ODBMSs)

The architecture must support ODBMS implementations and client interfaces to achieve these.

B.2 Roles for the ORB and ODBMS

The ORB and the ODBMS are different. The ODBMS's role in the OMG environment is to support definition, creation, and manipulation with the services of persistence, transactions, recovery, and concurrent sharing for application objects varying from the smallest units (e.g., words in a word processor, cells or formula terms in a spreadsheet) to the largest (e.g., documents, systems). Many applications desire these services to include, within a single vendor product, transparent distribution in a heterogeneous mixture of platforms and other services such as versioning and security.

Note that we define ODBMS according to the services it provides, not according to any particular implementation of those services. Radically different implementations are possible, including not only traditional ODBMS approaches, but also file-based approaches, each offering different levels of services and trade-offs.

The ORB provides a larger-scale set of services across heterogeneous vendors and products; e.g., it allows clients to use multiple ODBMSs. The service it provides is behavior invocation, or method dispatch. In contrast, the ODBMS provides a single-vendor capability and only a specific set of services rather than arbitrary ones; however, those services include more detailed capabilities of high-performance, fine-grained persistence that are used directly within applications to support millions of primitive objects. The ORB, when it needs persistence services, could choose to implement them via use of an ODBMS. The ODBMS services may be invoked via the ORB.

B.3 Issues

Here we describe some of the key issues that this architecture must address. Since the ODBMS supports millions of fine-grained objects used directly by the applications, it must provide high-performance access to those objects. The pertinent characteristic differentiating large- and small-grain objects is access time. If an application is accessing only one or two objects (e.g., open a spreadsheet document), there is little concern for the time to communicate across networks through the ORB. However, if the application is accessing thousands or millions of objects (e.g., formulae and variables in cells in the spreadsheet), system overhead becomes a significant factor as perceived by the user.

In many cases this means access time that is comparable to native in-memory object usage. To provide this, the ODBMS must be able to move objects as necessary in the distributed environment and cache them locally in the address space of the application, if desired, and in efficient format.

Since the ODBMS objects are those used primarily within the application, it is desirable to support an interface that is natural and direct to the user.

Examples of applications and object granularities for which ODBMS services must be available and efficient include spreadsheets; word processors; documents of these; primitive elements within these such as cells, formulae, variables, words, phrases, and formatting specifications; network managers with objects representing machines, users, and sessions; resource allocation schemes; CAD and CAM with objects such as circuits and gates and pins, routing traces, form features, bezier curves, finite element mesh nodes, edges and faces, tool paths, simulation, and analysis support; financial portfolio analysis; and so on. There may be millions of such objects, in complex interconnected networks of relationships.

The interfaces to those objects must be defined in such a way as to allow ORB access when appropriate (e.g., for cross-database-vendor object relationships) or direct use of the ODBMS (e.g., for objects with no need to publish themselves for public use through the ORB). This should be done with a single interface to allow transparency to the client and to allow the client to choose to vary functionality as desired.

The ODBMS acts as manager of many objects, so the architecture and interfaces must allow such assignment of responsibilities. The ODBMS can provide distribution of objects among multiple and potentially heterogeneous platforms, so the architecture and implementation must allow this functionality to be relegated to the ODBMS.

The ORB and other OMG components (service providers, library facilities, service users, etc.) may need the services of persistence, or management of objects that exist beyond process lifetimes, for various kinds of objects, including type-defining objects and instances of these. It is desirable, architecturally, to consolidate common services in a common shared component. The architecture must allow use of an ODBMS for this purpose in order to take advantage both of the capabilities it provides and integration with other OMG components using the same services.

As mentioned above, different ODBMS implementation approaches must be supported. The architecture and the OMG interfaces must provide a single interface (or set of interfaces) that allows use of a wide variety of such implementations. A single interface allows users to choose which implementation to use and when. This should cover not only full ODBMS implementations but other approaches with partial functionality, such as file management approaches.

In addition to direct use of an ODBMS through an interface such as that defined in the ODMG-93 specification, an ODBMS could be decomposed in order to implement a number of semi-independent *services*, such as persistence, transactions, relationships, and versions. The OMG Object Services Task Force is defining such services. This is an area for future work by the object database vendors.

In addition to the ORB and users of the ORB accessing ODBMSs, it is also the case that an ODBMS may be a client of the ORB. The ODBMS may want to use the ORB services such as location and naming (for distributed name services) or may use the ORB in order to access other ODBMSs, thus allowing heterogeneous ODBMS access. Current ODBMSs provide object identifiers that work only within one vendor's products, sometimes only within one database. The ORB object references could serve as a common denominator that allows selected object references and invocations in an ODBMS to span database boundaries (via encapsulating ODBMS object identifiers within ORB object references).

B.4 ODBMS as an Object Manager

The ORB acts as a communication mechanism to provide distributed, transparent dispatching of requests to objects among applications and service providers. The ODBMS acts as manager of a collection of objects, most of which are not directly registered as objects to the ORB, some of which can be very small (fine-grained) application objects, and for which high-speed transparent distributed access must be supported.

If every ODBMS object that an application wanted to reference were individually registered with the ORB or if every request to those objects in the ODBMS went through the ORB Basic Object Adaptor, the overhead would be unacceptable. This is equivalent to saying that every test of a bit of data or change of an integer must invoke the overhead of an RPC mechanism. Instead, the application should have the flexibility to choose which objects and which granularities are in fact known to the ORB, when requests to those objects go through the ORB, and be able to change this choice from time to time.

To achieve this maximum flexibility, we specify that the ODBMS has the capability to manage objects unknown or known to the ORB, to register subspaces of object identifiers with the ORB (to allow the ORB to handle requests to all of the objects in an ODBMS without the registration of each individual object), and to provide direct access to the objects it manages. For the objects unknown to the ORB, this direct access is provided via an ORB request to a containing object (e.g., a database), which then makes those objects directly available to the application. This provides consistency with and participation in the ORB environment and still provides the ODBMS with the ability to move objects around the distributed environment, cache them as appropriate, and provide efficient access.

For objects that the ODBMS has registered with the ORB, it may choose either to let requests to them execute the normal ORB mechanism or request from the ORB that any requests to those objects be passed to the ODBMS, perhaps for some period of time. Requests to such objects, whether through the ORB or directly to the ODBMS, must produce the same effect and be compatible with other users employing both mechanisms. In this way the ODBMS can provide consistency with the ORB and still coordinate with direct object requests.

The currently adopted OMG CORBA document provides for normal object access via the Basic Object Adaptor (BOA). For complete generality, flexibility, and interoperability, it executes via an interprocess mechanism (RPC for short) for every dispatch of every method. An extension is the Library Object Adaptor (LOA) that allows direct, considerably faster access to objects. After the first invocation (via the usual ORB mechanism), or through a compile-time optimization, a direct link is established to the object. Later access by the client to the object is then direct until the client notifies the ORB that it has released the object. We offer a new type of Object Adaptor, the Object Database Adaptor (ODA), to provide the ability to register a subspace of object identifiers and to allow access (including direct access) to the objects as if they had been individually registered.

The ODA provides a mechanism to register a subspace of object identifiers with the ORB rather than having to register all objects in the ODBMS. From the client's point of view, the objects in the registered subspace appear just as any other ORB-accessible objects, with the same interface. The ODA should allow for the use of direct access (as in the LOA) to improve the performance of ORB/ODBMS applications.

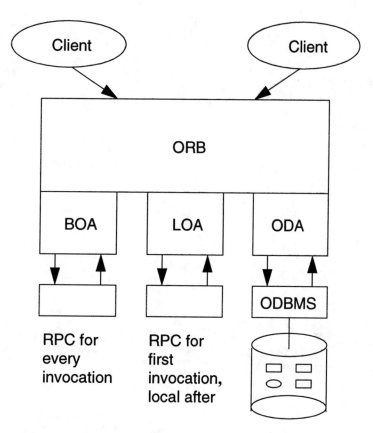

Figure B-1. ODBMS as Object Manager in OMG ORB Architecture

Index